Mastering TOEIC® Test-taking Skills

TOEIC®
Analyst

Second Edition

Anne Taylor

CONTENTS

The TOEIC® Reading Section

Practice Test

Transcripts and Answer Key

INTRODUCTION

TOEIC® Analyst Second Edition is designed to help students prepare for the TOEIC® by giving them practice with both question formats commonly found on the TOEIC® and strategies for analyzing the answer choices typically found on the test. The units in this book are organized according to skill (listening or reading) and task types (picture description, questions and responses, short conversations, short talks, incomplete sentences, incomplete texts, and reading comprehension). These tasks are then subdivided into common question types with each type explained in detail to help students focus on how to approach questions of different natures.

The basic principles of this book derive from proven test preparation techniques. The TOEIC® (Test of English for International Communication) is, after all, a standardized test created by ETS(Educational Testing Service), and the test shares many similarities with other ETS products. This book simply gives strategic test preparation techniques tailored to the unique content of the TOEIC® and the special nature of test takers for this test.

Accordingly, this book contains a number of practice questions organized by question type to allow you to practice the strategies and techniques of the TOEIC®. In addition, you will find two practice test included in this book designed to simulate the actual TOEIC®. It is recommended you take the practice test after you have completed the other materials in this book and are ready for a timed, full-length exam. To get the most benefit from the two practice tests, try to take them under exam conditions following the time limits set for the actual test.

As a final note, view the TOEIC® as a challenge. The test does not assess how smart you are or even how well you actually speak English. It only assesses how well you take the TOEIC® itself. Learn as much as you can, adopt a strategic approach and practice intelligently and you can achieve your TOEIC® goals.

The TOEIC®
Listening Section

The Listening Comprehension Section of the TOEIC® test consists of four parts: Picture Description, Questions and Responses, Short Conversations, and Short Talks. There are a total of one hundred questions. All questions relate to recorded materials. You must listen to the recording in order to answer the questions. You will have forty-five minutes to complete the Listening Comprehension Section. The timing of each part of this section is controlled by the audio tape recording.

You must follow along with the tape to answer the questions.

Part 1	Picture Description	10 questions
Part 2	Questions and Responses	30 questions
Part 3	Short Conversations	30 questions
Part 4	Short Talks	30 questions
Listening Total		100 questions

Picture Description

1

This section of the TOEIC® checks how well you can describe the given picture. First, identify what the picture focuses on, and then try to think of vocabulary related to it. Using that, try to form a possible statement that you think is appropriate for the picture. Note that no inferences are needed. In other words, if something is not clear from the picture, do not assume it is true simply because it seems reasonable. The correct answer should describe what can clearly be seen in the picture.

Test-taking Tips

✓ Don't read the directions for this section unless it is your first time taking the test.

✓ Preview the picture before you hear the statements.

✓ Determine the focus or main idea of the picture; ignore minor elements of the picture. Remember the correct answer always describes the main action or subject of the picture and is always in the present continuous or simple present tense.

✓ When listening to the statements, eliminate obviously wrong answers. This will help you guess quickly, if you are not sure.

Question Types

Type 1 — Location Questions
Type 2 — Action Questions
Type 3 — Situation Questions
Type 4 — Similar-Sounding Word Questions

Question Type 1

Location Questions

Questions of this sort often deal with the position of one person or thing in relation to someone or something else, so you should pay careful attention to the prepositions used in the statements you hear. Following is a list of some common prepositions for the location category:

> *above, against, among, at, at the back of, at the end of, atop, before, behind, below, beneath, between, by, close to, in, inside, in front of, near, next to, on, on top of, over, under*

Look at the following picture and the sentences next to it. Each sentence contains a commonly used preposition for location. In this example, all four sentences are possible. Of course, in the sample test question below, there is only one correct answer.

He is sitting at the kitchen table.

The woman is standing next to the man.

The banner is hanging behind the woman.

There is a cake on the table.

The woman is ------- the man.

Focus on:

woman

man

~~**eating**~~

~~**flowers**~~

next to

(A) There is a vase of flowers on the table.
(B) The cake is between the man and the woman.
(C) The woman is next to the man.
(D) The man is eating cake in the kitchen.

1.

Focus on:
papers
~~telephone~~
desk
~~computer~~
on

There are a lot of papers ------- the desk.

2.

Focus on:
suitcase
conveyor belt
on
~~airport~~

The man's suitcase is ------- the conveyor belt.

3.

Focus on:
above
helicopter
~~pilot~~
city

There is a helicopter ------- the city.

4.

Focus on:
~~passenger~~
on the corner
people
street

There are many people ------- the corner of the street.

PART 1
Picture Description

Type 1	Location Questions
Type 2	Action Questions
Type 3	Situation Questions
Type 4	Similar-Sounding Word Questions

TRANSCRIPTS

1. (A) There is a telephone on the woman's desk.
   (B) The woman is sitting behind the computer.
   (C) The woman is inside a store.
   (D) There are a lot of papers on the desk.

2. (A) The plane has arrived at the airport.
   (B) The man's suitcase is on the conveyor belt.
   (C) A man is meeting his friend at the airport.
   (D) The man is looking in his new suitcase.

3. (A) There is a helicopter above the city.
   (B) The pilot is landing in the city.
   (C) There are two pilots in the helicopter.
   (D) The helicopter is between the cities.

4. (A) There is no passenger in the car.
   (B) A passenger is getting in the car.
   (C) The car is parked on the sidewalk.
   (D) There are many people on the corner of the street.

PART 1

Picture Description

Type 1   Location Questions

Type 2   Action Questions

Type 3   Situation Questions

Type 4   Similar-Sounding
               Word Questions

Question Type 2

Action Questions

Keep in mind that the correct answer to a question of the action category can be in either the active or the passive form. The active form is usually a statement in the present continuous (i.e., *be + V-ing*). The passive is composed of *be + V-ed* participle of the main verb. Following is a list of common action verbs:

i. active

cleaning, crossing, cutting, drawing, drinking, eating, holding, jogging, listening, loading, (un)locking, making, packing, playing, pouring, pulling, pushing, selling, setting, sitting, speaking, stretching, sweeping, talking, typing, walking, watching, watering, working, wrapping, writing

ii. passive

being + cleaned, cleared, displayed, dug up, handed, locked, painted, planted, piled, served, set up, towed, walked, washed, watered, wrapped

Look at the following picture and the sentences next to it. Each sentence contains a commonly used action verb in either the active or passive form.

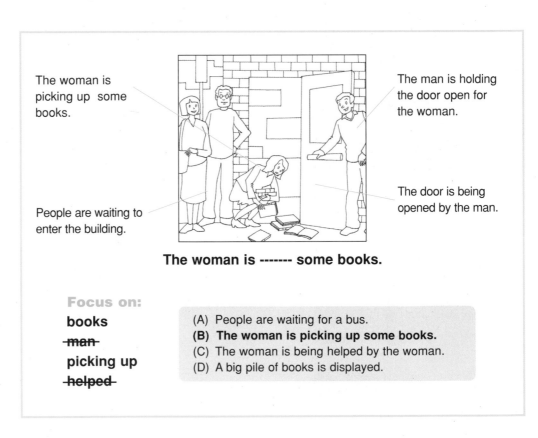

The woman is picking up some books.

The man is holding the door open for the woman.

People are waiting to enter the building.

The door is being opened by the man.

The woman is ------- some books.

Focus on:

books

~~man~~

picking up

~~helped~~

(A) People are waiting for a bus.
(B) **The woman is picking up some books.**
(C) The woman is being helped by the woman.
(D) A big pile of books is displayed.

PART 1

Picture Description

Type 1 Location Questions
Type 2 Action Questions
Type 3 Situation Questions
Type 4 Similar-Sounding
       Word Questions

1.

Focus on:
~~stopping~~
worn
helmet

A helmet is ------- by the rider.

2.

Focus on:
taught
teacher
students
~~chatting~~

The students are ------- by the teacher.

3.

Focus on:
walking
platform
woman
~~train~~

A woman is ------- along the platform.

4.

Focus on:
map
looking
~~car~~

The man and woman are ------- at a map.

TRANSCRIPTS

1. (A) The rider is holding a
       helmet.
   (B) The rider is stopping his
       motorcycle.
   (C) A helmet is being worn by
       the rider.
   (D) The motorcycle is being
       carried by the rider.

2. (A) The class is chatting.
   (B) The teacher is asking
       the student to stand up.
   (C) The student is teaching
       the teacher.
   (D) The students are being
       taught by the teacher.

3. (A) A woman is being walked
       along the platform.
   (B) A woman is walking
       along the platform.
   (C) The train is being driven
       by a woman.
   (D) The woman is getting on
       the train.

4. (A) The map is being folded
       by the man and woman.
   (B) They are driving a car.
   (C) The man and woman
       are looking at a map.
   (D) The car is being driven
       fast.

11

PART 1

Picture Description

Type 1 Location Questions
Type 2 Action Questions
Type 3 Situation Questions
Type 4 Similar-Sounding
          Word Questions

Question Type 3

Situation Questions

This category asks about the condition of things in the picture. With the two categories below, you should try identifying what the picture focuses on and imagining a description of the picture before the statements are read. Following is a list of common adjectives for the situation category:

i. past participle forms used as adjectives

arranged, broken, chained, cleared, closed, crowded, crushed, deserted, displayed, equipped, (un)loaded, locked, occupied, parked, piled, posted, scattered, seated, spread, stacked, tied

ii. adjectives

asleep, beautiful, bent, bright, clean, dark, dirty, empty, flat, full, happy, heavy, high, light, long, open, rainy, round, tall, sad, straight, wet

Look at the following picture and the sentences next to it. Each sentence contains a commonly used adjective.

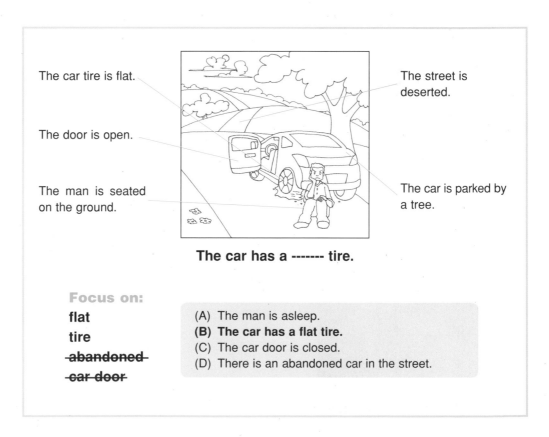

The car tire is flat.

The door is open.

The man is seated on the ground.

The street is deserted.

The car is parked by a tree.

The car has a ------- tire.

Focus on:

flat

tire

~~abandoned~~

~~car door~~

(A) The man is asleep.
(B) The car has a flat tire.
(C) The car door is closed.
(D) There is an abandoned car in the street.

1.

Focus on:
flowers
hanging
pots
~~roof~~

The ------- pots have flowers in them.

2.

Focus on:
seated
woman
~~barn~~

A woman is ------- on the car.

3.

Focus on:
mail box
closed
~~open~~

The mail box is -------.

4.

Focus on:
sink
full
~~hot~~

The sinks are ------- of water.

PART 1

Picture Description

Type 1	Location Questions
Type 2	Action Questions
Type 3	Situation Questions
Type 4	Similar-Sounding Word Questions

TRANSCRIPTS

1. (A) The flowers are growing between two houses.
   (B) The benches are in front of the pretty flowers.
   (C) The hanging pots have flowers in them.
   (D) There are lots of flowers on the roof of the house.

2. (A) The car is parked by a barn.
   (B) A man is driving the car.
   (C) A woman is seated on the car.
   (D) The car has broken down.

3. (A) The mail box is full of newspapers.
   (B) A man is delivering mail.
   (C) The mail box is open.
   (D) The mail box is closed.

4. (A) The glasses are broken.
   (B) The sinks are full of water.
   (C) The sinks are empty.
   (D) The water is hot.

Question Type 4

Similar-Sounding Word Questions

Incorrect choices often include words that sound similar to the key words of the correct answers. You might wish to keep a journal of similar-sounding words that sometimes confuse you. Examples of words that might easily be confused include:

i. **words that have little sound difference, such as _walk_ and _work_, or that rhyme, such as _station_ and _nation_.**

ball/bowl	lean/learn	pine/fine	talk/take
bike/hike	light/right	player/prayer	there/they're
clean/lean	lock/rock	playing/plane	try/tie
coach/couch	low/row	pool/pull	wait/weigh
hitting/fitting	mail/rail	poor/four	walk/work
just/adjust	meal/wheel	possible/impossible	west/rest
lake/rake	on the/under	rag/bag	wheel/will
lamp/ramp	peach/speech	selling/sailing	
law/raw	peel/pill	shopping/chopping	

ii. **words with the same root, prefix, or suffix, such as _example_/_examine_**

agree/disagree	relay/delay	tie/untie
appear/disappear	reread/relayed	tire/retire
close/enclose	rest/arrest	type/retype
extract/exhale	similar/dissimilar	underworked/underused
just/adjust	terrible/terrific	undrinkable/unthinkable

Look at the following picture and the sentences next to it. Each sentence contains a commonly confused word.

The woman is holding a ball.

There is a bowl on the desk.

The lamp is on the woman's right.

The man is taking a photo.

The woman is talking on the telephone.

The woman is sitting by a lamp.

The woman is ------- on the phone.

Focus on:

talking

~~bowl~~

~~photo~~

(A) The woman is holding a bowl.
(B) The woman is talking on the phone.
(C) The woman is taking the photo.
(D) The man is talking on the phone.

1.

The man is ------- the woman.

Focus on:

man
~~couch~~
coaching
~~sitting~~

2.

The man is ------- watches.

Focus on:

selling
~~sailing~~
~~watching~~

3.

There is a ------- in front of the hut.

Focus on:

ramp
~~lamp~~
~~sea~~
hut

4.

The man is ------- for a train.

Focus on:

waiting
~~weighing~~
~~tray~~

PART 1

Picture Description

Type 1	Location Questions
Type 2	Action Questions
Type 3	Situation Questions
Type 4	Similar-Sounding Word Questions

TRANSCRIPTS

1. (A) The man is sitting on a couch.
   (B) The man is coaching the woman.
   (C) The woman is leaning.
   (D) The woman is standing next to a couch.

2. (A) The man is sailing.
   (B) The man is watching a sale.
   (C) The man is selling watches.
   (D) The man is tired.

3. (A) There is a lamp in front of the hut.
   (B) The ramp leads to the sea.
   (C) There is a ramp in front of the hut.
   (D) The sky is getting cloudy.

4. (A) The man is weighing a train.
   (B) The man is waiting for a train.
   (C) The man is holding a tray.
   (D) It is starting to rain.

Sample Test: PART 1

Choose the statement that best describes what you see in the picture.

1.

2.

3.

4.

5.

6.

7.

8.

9.

10.

Transcripts: PART 1

1. (A) The man is sleeping at his desk.
   (B) The man is typing at his desk.
   (C) The man is attending a meeting.
   (D) The man is drinking tea.

2. (A) There are TVs stacked up on the shelves.
   (B) There is a microwave oven tacked up on the wall.
   (C) There are microwave ovens on the shelves.
   (D) There are many books on the shelves.

3. (A) The man is standing in front of some picture frames.
   (B) The man is selling fans.
   (C) The man is standing beside a bus stop.
   (D) The man is satisfied with a fan.

4. (A) The woman is buying vegetables.
   (B) The man is going grocery shopping.
   (C) The woman is selling vegetables.
   (D) The woman is buying shoes.

5. (A) The woman is carrying a suitcase.
   (B) The woman is folding her umbrella.
   (C) An umbrella is being held by the woman.
   (D) The man is sleeping.

6. (A) The woman is getting in a taxi.
   (B) The woman is talking to the driver.
   (C) The woman is being called.
   (D) The woman's arm is held up.

7. (A) The woman is sitting beside a computer.
   (B) The woman is sitting at a computer.
   (C) The woman is sitting next to a computer.
   (D) The woman is sitting at the back of a computer.

8. (A) The three men are happy.
   (B) The three men are asleep.
   (C) The three men look disappointed.
   (D) The three men are angry.

9. (A) The man has dropped his jacket.
   (B) The man is holding a briefcase.
   (C) The man is sitting outside.
   (D) There is a cat on the man's lap.

10. (A) The people are listening to the woman.
    (B) The woman is reading a letter.
    (C) The people are standing in a meeting room.
    (D) The woman is attending a concert.

PART 2 | Questions and Responses

Strategies

This section of the TOEIC® checks whether you can make an appropriate response to a given question. Consider in what respect the given responses are appropriate for the question, and guess how the given incorrect choices are inappropriate. Remember incorrect choices often contain a word or phrase from the question, so don't be misled by mere repetition of words or phrases.

Test-taking Tips

✓ Once you find a possible correct response, do not wait until all the choices are spoken.

✓ Check that there is no problem with tense and/or subject-verb agreement.

✓ Keep in mind that *wh*-questions cannot be answered with *yes* or *no*.

✓ When the question begins with a *wh*-word, be careful not to confuse the word with something else. For example, *how* might be confused with *who* or even *where*.

Question Types

Type 1 — *Who* Questions
Type 2 — *When* Questions
Type 3 — *Where* Questions
Type 4 — *What* Questions
Type 5 — *How* Questions
Type 6 — *Why* Questions
Type 7 — *Yes/No* Questions
Type 8 — Choice Questions
Type 9 — Statements

TIPS

- Responses (A), (B), and (C) contain relevant information: the name of a writer, and expressions that show preference such as "love," "favorite writer," and "admire."
- Responses (D) and (E) contain irrelevant information: the name of a painter, and a "yes" reply.

TIPS

- (A), (B), and (C) tell us who didn't finish lunch: "I didn't (finish lunch)," "John didn't (finish lunch)," and "It was John (who didn't finish lunch)."
- (D) answers the question "Who didn't bring lunch?" while (E) answers the question "Why?"

Question Type 1

Who Questions

Who questions usually ask about a person, a group, an organization, or a job title. Keep in mind that *who* questions are occasionally negative, as in *Who is not coming to the party?*

i) Who is your favorite writer?

Correct responses:

(A) I love Ernest Hemingway.
(B) My favorite writer is Ernest Hemingway.
(C) Ernest Hemingway. I admire him.

Incorrect responses:

(D) My favorite painter is Picasso.
(E) Yes, I like Ernest Hemingway.

ii) Who didn't finish lunch?

Correct responses:

(A) I didn't.
(B) John didn't.
(C) It was John.

Incorrect responses:

(D) Nobody brought lunch.
(E) Because it tasted awful.

Warm-ups

1. Whom did you get that message from?

   (A) The manager of the payroll department.
   (B) Yesterday, we talked about it.
   (C) John didn't know about the message.

2. Whose jacket is that?

   (A) It was made in China.
   (B) It's made of cotton.
   (C) It's mine.

3. Who didn't attend the meeting yesterday?

   (A) John forgot about the meeting.
   (B) It finished late.
   (C) The personnel manager.

Question Type 2
When Questions

When questions always ask about time. Therefore, look for time expressions such as the following:

> *during, at ... o'clock, ago, on Monday, at night, in the morning, yesterday, next week, in a few days, when, by Friday, etc.*

Note that it is sometimes possible to reply to a *When* question using *When*.

i) When did you get that message?

Correct responses:
(A) I got it yesterday.
(B) Yesterday morning.
(C) Three days ago.

Incorrect responses:
(D) I found it on the desk.
(E) I got it from the manager.

TIPS

* While responses (A), (B), and (C) all contain time expressions, (D) and (E) lack any time reference.

ii) When would you like to have dinner?

Correct responses:
(A) How about six o'clock?
(B) Any time you are available.
(C) When all the guests arrive.

Incorrect responses:
(D) How about at a Chinese restaurant?
(E) No, thank you. I'm full.

TIPS

* Again, (D), and (E) both lack time expressions. (D) could be a good response to "Where would you like to have dinner?"

Warm-ups

1. When did you get up this morning?

    (A) At dawn.
    (B) Yes, I got up early this morning.
    (C) Because of a loud noise.

2. When do you think you can finish the report?

    (A) I didn't think it was difficult.
    (B) It will be done by the third.
    (C) I'm looking forward to it.

3. When are you visiting the Hong Kong branch?

    (A) I'm going in a few days.
    (B) Yes, I am visiting it soon.
    (C) I didn't go to Hong Kong this time.

TIPS

• Although (D) contains a prepositional phrase, "grocery store" is obviously not appropriate for this question. (E) does not tell us "where."

TIPS

• Responses (A), (B), and (C) are all logical replies to someone asking for directions. Responses (D) and (E) have no relation to the content of the question.

Question Type 3

Where Questions

Where questions almost always ask a location, and so often include prepositional phrases. Remember, however, that the preposition is occasionally omitted.

i) Where did you get your hair cut?

Correct responses:
(A) At the new salon next door.
(B) I went to Bill's.
(C) At Jill's, as usual.

Incorrect responses:
(D) At a grocery store.
(E) I got it cut too short.

ii) Where do we go from here?

Correct responses:
(A) Turn right and go three blocks.
(B) I think we make the next left.
(C) Well, let's take a look at the map.

Incorrect responses:
(D) You're absolutely right.
(E) I don't know how to drive.

Warm-ups

1. Where is a shoe store near here?

    (A) Leather shoes last longer.
    (B) The shop has a large selection of shoes.
    (C) Down the street, past the church.

2. Where's your new office?

    (A) I'm in the cafeteria.
    (B) On the fourth floor.
    (C) It's too big.

3. Where do you usually buy your coffee?

    (A) It's rather expensive these days.
    (B) At a little store next to the supermarket.
    (C) I don't drink coffee at work.

Question Type 4
What Questions

PART 2

Questions and Responses

Type 1   *Who* Questions
Type 2   *When* Questions
Type 3   *Where* Questions
Type 4   *What* Questions
Type 5   *How* Questions
Type 6   *Why* Questions
Type 7   *Yes/No* Questions
Type 8   Choice Questions
Type 9   Statements

The scope of *what* questions, regarding the type of information asked, is quite broad. Attention should therefore be paid to the vocabulary and grammar in both the questions and the responses. Note that verb tenses and pronouns can be very important for making the correct choice.

i) What are these boxes for?

Correct responses:

(A) They're for the books.
(B) They are to be used as seats.
(C) To keep old documents in.

Incorrect responses:

(D) The box was going to be recycled.
(E) They were put there yesterday.

TIPS

- The question asks about the purpose or function of the boxes. However, (D) and (E) do not address the function of the boxes. Also, their tenses do not match the question.

ii) What happened to your son?

Correct responses:

(A) He sprained his ankle.
(B) He caught a cold walking in the rain.
(C) Nothing. Why do you ask?

Incorrect responses:

(D) He's about to start college.
(E) Nothing happened to her.

TIPS

- The key points to note in this question are "happened" (simple past tense) and "son." Response (D) is a future form and therefore inappropriate. Response (E) is incorrect because of the pronoun "her."

Warm-ups

1. What time does the movie start?

   (A) It will last about two hours.
   (B) There is no theater here.
   (C) I don't know. Let's look at the timetable.

2. What does your sister do?

   (A) He works at a bank.
   (B) She's a salesperson.
   (C) She can help you any time you want.

3. What are you going to tell Mr. Runfeld when he calls?

   (A) He is going to call this afternoon.
   (B) I'll think of something to say, so don't worry.
   (C) I couldn't answer the phone.

Answer Key   1 C   2 B   3 B

TIPS

• Responses (A), (B), and (C) all describe the process or manner in which the speaker opened an item. Response (D) answers "when" and (E) suggests the item has not been opened yet.

TIPS

• The question requires a response which talks about the speaker's opinion of the teacher's character or qualities. Therefore, (D) and (E) are not appropriate choices.

Question Type 5

How Questions

There are three types of *How* questions:

• asking about the process by, or manner in, which something is done
e.g., *How did you get here? How are you going to convince him?*

• asking about the quality or condition of something
e.g., *How is your soup? How is your father these days?*

• combining *how* with an adjective or adverb to inquire about the degree or quantity of something
e.g., *How much time is left? How quickly did you finish?*

i) How did you open this?

Correct responses:

(A) I used Mike's key.
(B) I just turned that handle.
(C) I had to pull quite hard.

Incorrect responses:

(D) I opened it a few minutes ago.
(E) We need a hammer.

ii) So, how is your teacher?

Correct responses:

(A) She's very strict.
(B) I don't like him very much.
(C) She knows her stuff.

Incorrect responses:

(D) He doesn't like French.
(E) I met her last year.

Warm-ups

1. How would you like your coffee?

   (A) No sugar, please.
   (B) Yes, I would like coffee.
   (C) I prefer coffee to tea.

2. How long have you been here?

   (A) About three and a half years.
   (B) It took three hours by bus.
   (C) I'm fine. How about you?

3. How long does it take to get to the town center from here?

   (A) There's a bus every thirty minutes.
   (B) No more than 20 minutes, if the traffic is light.
   (C) I'm driving to the town center tonight.

Question Type 6
Why Questions

Why questions usually inquire about the cause or reason for something. They are often found in the negative form. Remember that answers to these questions often include words like *because* or *due to*, but they may also simply state the reason. Be careful, though, if you hear *Why don't you...?* or *Why don't we...?* The question may in fact be a suggestion rather than a request.

i) Why did the national team lose so badly?

Correct responses:

(A) They didn't prepare well enough.
(B) Because their best player was injured.
(C) It was due to their inexperience.

Incorrect responses:

(D) They lost 8-1.
(E) Better luck next time.

- The response needs to be a reason why the team lost. Response (D) gives us the result of the game, and (E) would be better suited as a response to a statement such as "The national team lost badly."

ii) Why don't we get together next week?

Correct responses:

(A) Sounds good.
(B) That's a great idea!
(C) OK. How about Wednesday, then?

Incorrect responses:

(D) I didn't have the time.
(E) The plans have yet to be made.

- Here the question is a suggestion or invitation to meet in the near future. Responses (A), (B), and (C) all show acceptance of the suggestion. Response (D) would be appropriate after meeting, while (E) has no relation to the question.

Warm-ups

1. Why do you think he didn't support our plan?

   (A) I don't think so at all.
   (B) He seems to dislike any new ideas.
   (C) You're right about that.

2. Why was he late for school?

   (A) It's not my fault.
   (B) I think he took the wrong bus.
   (C) School finished at 5:00.

3. Why didn't you tell me that he had resigned?

   (A) I thought that you already knew.
   (B) Yes, he resigned yesterday.
   (C) Because it's a hot day.

TIPS

• Response (D) "I hate getting up early," is not a definitive yes/no answer, and it is therefore inappropriate. While (E) is a "yes" reply, it doesn't answer the question asked here.

TIPS

• Note that it is possible to reply with another question as in (C). Check that the response matches the question—(D) is wrong because it mentions time, not the mode of transportation. In (E) the reply mentions a bus, but the question is about a taxi.

Question Type 7

Yes/No Questions

Yes/No questions will ask opinions or preferences, request something, make a suggestion, or make an offer. These are quite often, but not always, answered with a *yes* or *no*. The questions usually begin with: *Are, Is, Do, Does, Did, Can, Could, Have, Will, Would, May, Shall,* or *Should*. They may also be in the form of tag questions (e.g., *You are coming with us, aren't you?*).

i) Do you get up early?

Correct responses:

(A) Only on weekdays.
(B) Yes, on weekdays.
(C) Not really. I usually get up quite late.

Incorrect responses:

(D) I hate getting up early.
(E) Yes, I promise.

ii) You generally take a taxi to work, don't you?

Correct responses:

(A) No, I usually take the subway.
(B) I used to, but these days I can't afford it.
(C) How did you know that?

Incorrect responses:

(D) Sometimes it takes about 10 minutes.
(E) Yes, I often take a bus to work.

Warm-ups

1. Didn't you go to the book fair?

    (A) Sure, if you want to.
    (B) I did, but I didn't stay long.
    (C) Yes, I didn't.

2. Are you going to attend the conference?

    (A) I guess so.
    (B) We were too late.
    (C) From the 2nd to the 5th.

3. Could you show me how this fax machine works?

    (A) It is a new fax machine.
    (B) Of course. It's very simple.
    (C) Has the fax already been sent?

Question Type 8

Choice Questions

PART 2

Questions and Responses

Type 1 *Who* Questions
Type 2 *When* Questions
Type 3 *Where* Questions
Type 4 *What* Questions
Type 5 *How* Questions
Type 6 *Why* Questions
Type 7 *Yes/No* Questions
Type 8 *Choice Questions*
Type 9 Statements

Choice questions ask you to choose between two alternatives which are always related to each other. Remember that these questions cannot be answered using *yes* or *no*. Look for the conjunction *or* in the questions.

i) Will he be arriving tonight or tomorrow?

Correct responses:

(A) He will get in tonight at about 7:00.
(B) Tomorrow, according to his secretary.
(C) He didn't say for sure.

Incorrect responses:

(D) Yes, he is going to be here.
(E) He will call us tomorrow.

ii) Have you finished the report, or are you still working on it?

Correct responses:

(A) I should have it done by tonight.
(B) I need another week to complete it.
(C) I'm still tied up with it.

Incorrect responses:

(D) I spoke to you yesterday.
(E) Yes, I certainly am.

TIPS

- The key words here are "arriving tonight or tomorrow." Response (D) does not address the issue of choice, and (E) does not inform us as to whether "he" will be arriving or not.

TIPS

- Responses (A) through (C) all refer to the degree of completion that the speaker has achieved, so they are all suitable responses. Responses (D) and (E) do not pertain to the question in any way.

Warm-ups

1. Are you going to buy a new computer or just continue using the old one?

    (A) Neither. I'm going to lease one.
    (B) Yes, I'd like one, thank you.
    (C) That's impossible. I can't afford a new one.

2. Which do you prefer, the yellow T-shirt or the blue one?

    (A) Yes, I like the blue one.
    (B) Neither.
    (C) Both of them are very cheap.

3. Is Joseph or Manuel going to present the proposal?

    (A) Yes, they are going to make the presentation.
    (B) Manuel said he would do it.
    (C) Well, I'd like to, but I'm busy.

PART 2

Questions and Responses

Type 1 *Who* Questions
Type 2 *When* Questions
Type 3 *Where* Questions
Type 4 *What* Questions
Type 5 *How* Questions
Type 6 *Why* Questions
Type 7 *Yes/No* Questions
Type 8 Choice Questions
Type 9 Statements

TIPS

• Expressions of concern or sympathy are the most appropriate choices here.

TIPS

• Expressions that show pleasure at the speaker's good news are the most suitable choices here.

Question Type 9

Statements

In some instances, the question is not an actual question, but rather a statement to which you have to match an appropriate response. This could be a common greeting or daily expression to which there is a set response in English. You will need to consider the context and draw upon logic to choose the correct reply.

i) I have a terrible headache.

Correct responses:

(A) That's too bad. I hope it goes away.
(B) Why don't you take some aspirin?
(C) Maybe you should take a rest.

Incorrect responses:

(D) That's wonderful news.
(E) It's getting cold, isn't it?

ii) I've been promoted to division head.

Correct responses:

(A) Congratulations! You deserve it.
(B) That's great. When do you start the position?
(C) Well, then we should celebrate.

Incorrect responses:

(D) That's not my problem.
(E) When is the next meeting?

Warm-ups

1. I've put the accounting files on your desk.

 (A) Thanks. I'll look at them later.
 (B) I haven't phoned yet.
 (C) It's going to be difficult to finish.

2. Thank you for taking the time to come here in person.

 (A) There are many people in this branch.
 (B) Don't mention it. It's my pleasure.
 (C) What do you feel like eating?

3. I've arranged the meeting for three o'clock on Thursday.

 (A) I don't enjoy meetings.
 (B) I have had a lot of phone calls today.
 (C) Good, I'll mark it on my planner.

Sample Test: PART 2

Listen to the questions and choose the best answer.

1. Mark your answer on your answer sheet.　　(A)　　(B)　　(C)
2. Mark your answer on your answer sheet.　　(A)　　(B)　　(C)
3. Mark your answer on your answer sheet.　　(A)　　(B)　　(C)
4. Mark your answer on your answer sheet.　　(A)　　(B)　　(C)
5. Mark your answer on your answer sheet.　　(A)　　(B)　　(C)
6. Mark your answer on your answer sheet.　　(A)　　(B)　　(C)
7. Mark your answer on your answer sheet.　　(A)　　(B)　　(C)
8. Mark your answer on your answer sheet.　　(A)　　(B)　　(C)
9. Mark your answer on your answer sheet.　　(A)　　(B)　　(C)
10. Mark your answer on your answer sheet.　　(A)　　(B)　　(C)
11. Mark your answer on your answer sheet.　　(A)　　(B)　　(C)
12. Mark your answer on your answer sheet.　　(A)　　(B)　　(C)
13. Mark your answer on your answer sheet.　　(A)　　(B)　　(C)
14. Mark your answer on your answer sheet.　　(A)　　(B)　　(C)
15. Mark your answer on your answer sheet.　　(A)　　(B)　　(C)
16. Mark your answer on your answer sheet.　　(A)　　(B)　　(C)
17. Mark your answer on your answer sheet.　　(A)　　(B)　　(C)
18. Mark your answer on your answer sheet.　　(A)　　(B)　　(C)
19. Mark your answer on your answer sheet.　　(A)　　(B)　　(C)
20. Mark your answer on your answer sheet.　　(A)　　(B)　　(C)
21. Mark your answer on your answer sheet.　　(A)　　(B)　　(C)
22. Mark your answer on your answer sheet.　　(A)　　(B)　　(C)
23. Mark your answer on your answer sheet.　　(A)　　(B)　　(C)
24. Mark your answer on your answer sheet.　　(A)　　(B)　　(C)
25. Mark your answer on your answer sheet.　　(A)　　(B)　　(C)
26. Mark your answer on your answer sheet.　　(A)　　(B)　　(C)
27. Mark your answer on your answer sheet.　　(A)　　(B)　　(C)
28. Mark your answer on your answer sheet.　　(A)　　(B)　　(C)
29. Mark your answer on your answer sheet.　　(A)　　(B)　　(C)
30. Mark your answer on your answer sheet.　　(A)　　(B)　　(C)

Transcripts: PART 2

1. How long has he been gone?
   (A) Until tomorrow.
   (B) For half an hour.
   (C) Next week.

2. I'm afraid I can't hear you.
   (A) I'm sorry. I'll speak louder.
   (B) Yes, I can come up now.
   (C) I really can't say.

3. Would you like to go now?
   (A) In a few minutes.
   (B) I go there every day.
   (C) I usually go by taxi.

4. How often do they update the computers?
   (A) Yes, they often do.
   (B) Two or three times a year.
   (C) About one or two weeks.

5. Why did you turn the air conditioner on?
   (A) It isn't working very well.
   (B) It's in good condition.
   (C) It's a little warm in here.

6. Didn't you used to work at Macy's with Sarah Davis?
   (A) When do we begin work?
   (B) Yes, that's right.
   (C) I certainly do.

7. Who is responsible for this?
   (A) I don't have it.
   (B) I believe Susan is.
   (C) No, I'm not.

8. I have a bit of a cold.
   (A) It's nearly spring.
   (B) You should take it easy.
   (C) That's a wonderful idea.

9. Whose briefcase is this?
   (A) It's my boss's.
   (B) They're probably lost.
   (C) His luggage is full.

10. Would you like tea or coffee?
    (A) It's fine, thanks.
    (B) Yes, please.
    (C) Coffee would be nice.

11. How many stories tall is that building?
    (A) About thirty-five.
    (B) I read it already.
    (C) Yes, it's quite high.

12. Did he fill out the form completely?
    (A) He forgot to sign and date it.
    (B) Once in a while it loses its shape.
    (C) Could I borrow your pen?

13. If you don't answer the letter, who will?
    (A) My assistant will.
    (B) Because I don't want to.
    (C) The answer is wrong.

14. When does the sale finish?
    (A) Yes, it has finished.
    (B) Office equipment is on sale.
    (C) It runs until next Friday.

15. Could you open these desk drawers for me?
    (A) I can't. They're stuck.
    (B) Sure, you can close them.
    (C) It opens at four o'clock.

16. When does your subscription expire?
    (A) In March.
    (B) For one year.
    (C) Twice a week.

17. When do you want to discuss my memo?
    (A) No, but I'll finish it by tomorrow.
    (B) I need to write several more pages.
    (C) How about this afternoon?

18. Where is Brian Ivan's desk?
    (A) It's at seven-fifty.
    (B) It's over there, by the window.
    (C) Certainly, just a moment.

19. Why isn't this working?

    (A) Did you plug it in?
    (B) Sure. It's really quite simple.
    (C) I'm on vacation.

20. What are you going to do with the old computers?

    (A) I'm donating them to a school.
    (B) They are old, aren't they?
    (C) They are mine.

21. Have you heard about the accident at the airport?

    (A) I'll be taking the next flight.
    (B) No, I haven't. What happened?
    (C) We ran into each other this afternoon.

22. Is Brenda making an announcement tonight?

    (A) I know she received an invitation.
    (B) The volume is a little low.
    (C) I think she's waiting until tomorrow.

23. We're going to be late.

    (A) I don't have time.
    (B) That's a good idea.
    (C) Let's call Mike and let him know.

24. Is this for Frank Green or Frank Venus?

    (A) Why don't you ask him?
    (B) I think it's for Mr. Green.
    (C) No, it isn't.

25. Where's the best place to take a client for lunch?

    (A) I usually go to the café on the corner.
    (B) I never eat lunch.
    (C) Yes, but I have no clients this week.

26. Have you been able to reach Eric?

    (A) There's no approval.
    (B) It's much too high.
    (C) No, the line is busy.

27. Where can I find information on American engineering schools?

    (A) The train schedule isn't posted.
    (B) Why don't you try the library?
    (C) My application was rejected.

28. What time does the meeting begin?

    (A) It's just a day late.
    (B) I've been waiting an hour.
    (C) At 3 o'clock.

29. Have you seen Jill recently?

    (A) Yes, just yesterday.
    (B) She was recently hired.
    (C) I don't know her very well.

30. Dolores Cohen is holding on line two. Can you take it?

    (A) Yes, two o'clock sounds fine.
    (B) No. Ask her to call me back.
    (C) I think it's time to let it go.

3 | Short Conversations

Strategies

This section of the TOEIC® includes three- or four-part dialogs between two people. First read the question along with the answer choices before the dialogs begin. You should try to find key words and the main idea so you can choose the correct statement quickly. Use your time wisely and preview the next question.

Test-taking Tips

✓ Don't be misled by mere repetition of a word or phrase from the text. All answer choices have been mentioned in the text, so listen carefully to how they are used in context.

✓ Remember the following frequently asked questions: the conversation topic, the relationship between people mentioned, the place in which the conversation takes place, or the activity people are engaged in.

✓ Try to listen for specific or suggested information: a specific time, a length of time, frequency, reason, intention, or conclusion.

Question Types

Type 1 — *Who* Questions
Type 2 — *When* Questions
Type 3 — *Where* Questions
Type 4 — *What* Questions
Type 5 — *How* Questions
Type 6 — *Why* Questions
Type 7 — *Which* Questions

Question Type 1

Who Questions

Who questions generally ask for information or details about a person, an organization, or a job title. The answer is likely to contain a noun phrase.

(Man)	Dinner's ready. Now we just have to wait for Sue and her new boyfriend.
(Woman)	Your sister seems to have a new boyfriend every month. What happened to Joe?
(Man)	He moved to California.
(Woman)	Really?

i) Who is coming to dinner?

Correct answers:
(A) The man's sister and her boyfriend
(B) Sue and her boyfriend

Incorrect answers:
(C) Someone from California
(D) The woman's ex-boyfriend
(E) Joe and Sue

TIPS

• We can understand from the conversation that the man's sister is named Sue and that she has a new boyfriend whose name we don't know. We also know that they are both coming to dinner. Therefore, (A) and (B) are both possible.

(Woman)	Did you send the fax to the Springfield office?
(Man)	Yes, and Andy Green said he had passed it on to his manager, Jeff.
(Woman)	I hope he replies soon.

ii) Who works in the Springfield office?

Correct answers:
(A) Jeff and Andy Green
(B) Andy Green and his manager

Incorrect answers:
(C) The woman
(D) The man
(E) Both the man and the woman

TIPS

• The content of the conversation indicates that the man and woman work in the same location. We understand that the Springfield office is a separate location where Jeff and Andy Green are both employed.

WARM-UP TRANSCRIPTS

1. (M) I've just made some coffee. Would anyone like a cup?
   (W) Not for me, but I'm sure Frank will have some.
   (M) Right. I'll take him a cup. I pass his desk on the way to mine.

2. (M) Where are the files for the Brookfield account? I need to read them before I leave tonight.
   (W) I haven't seen them, but you might want to ask someone in the records office. I'd call Janet or Sam if I were you.
   (M) Hmm, you are probably right. I don't know Janet, but Sam is always helpful. I have his number on my desk.

Warm-ups

1. Who will the man give a cup of coffee to?

   (A) The woman
   (C) Frank

   (B) The people at their desks
   (D) Frank and the woman

2. Who will the man call?

   (A) The woman
   (C) Janet

   (B) His boss
   (D) Sam

Question Type 2

When Questions

PART 3

Short Conversations

Type 1	*Who* Questions
Type 2	*When* Questions
Type 3	*Where* Questions
Type 4	*What* Questions
Type 5	*How* Questions
Type 6	*Why* Questions
Type 7	*Which* Questions

When questions focus on details about time. Therefore, you should listen for words and expressions related to time such as *at three o'clock, at two fifteen, on Friday, on Thursday night, in the morning, in a few hours, two days ago*, etc. These questions can refer to a present, past, or future event. Note, also, that the answer does not always include a preposition.

(Man)	The lecture starts at 8:45. We should have left already! We're going to be late yet again. Why do you always wait until the last minute?
(Woman)	What are you talking about? It's 7:00 now, and it only takes 30 minutes to get there. We still have plenty of time.
(Man)	I know, but the best seats will be taken before we get there. I want to get a good seat so that I can hear the speakers well.

i) When does the lecture start?

Correct answers:
(A) In one and three quarter hours
(B) 8:45
(C) A quarter to nine

Incorrect answers:
(D) 7:30
(E) 8:30
(F) In thirty minutes

TIPS

- The time difference between now and 8:45 is one and three quarter hours (A). The man states that the lecture starts at 8:45; in other words a quarter to nine, therefore (B) and (C) are correct. It is 7:00 now. We hear "30 minutes" but it refers to "how long," not "when."

(Woman)	Why does the photocopier always jam when I'm in a hurry? I need to make 100 copies of this before the meeting. This happens every time I need something quickly.
(Man)	Well, it's only 9:00 a.m. now. It'll only take about 20 minutes to make 100 copies. When do you need them?
(Woman)	Well, that's the problem. The meeting is supposed to start in 10 minutes.

ii) When does the meeting start?

Correct answers:
(A) At 9:10 a.m.
(B) In ten minutes

Incorrect answers:
(C) Hours
(D) In 20 minutes
(E) At 9:00 a.m.

TIPS

- Although we hear the words "hundred," "20 minutes," and "9:00 a.m." in the conversation, they do not refer to the meeting time. We know it is 9:00 a.m. now, and that the meeting starts in 10 minutes, making (A) and (B) appropriate choices.

Warm-ups

1. When is the man's flight?

   (A) Wednesday morning
   (B) In half an hour
   (C) Wednesday afternoon
   (D) On time

2. When will the cafeteria be closed?

   (A) From 8:00 to 3:00
   (B) From 3:00 to 6:00
   (C) From 6:00 to 9:00
   (D) From November 3rd

WARM-UP TRANSCRIPTS

1. (W) You are leaving on Wednesday morning, aren't you? Have you remembered to ask Mike to book a taxi to the airport?
   (M) Oh, no. Actually, I'm leaving Wednesday afternoon, and Patrick Byrne said he could give me a ride. He has to deliver something nearby. So I don't need a taxi.
   (W) Well, I hope Patrick's on time. The last time he gave me a ride, he was over half an hour late.

2. (M) Did you hear that the cafeteria is expanding its hours of operation?
   (W) No. To be honest, I never go there because it's always closed when I need something to eat.
   (M) Right, well most people felt the same way as you, so from November 3rd it is going to be open from 8:00 to 3:00, and then again from 6:00 to 9:00 p.m. It'll be a lot more convenient.

PART 3

Short Conversations

Type 1	*Who* Questions
Type 2	*When* Questions
Type 3	*Where* Questions
Type 4	*What* Questions
Type 5	*How* Questions
Type 6	*Why* Questions
Type 7	*Which* Questions

TIPS

• The woman had an accident over the weekend, so (E) is impossible. She needed to have her car repaired Monday after 9:00 a.m., therefore (A) and (B) are appropriate. She missed the meeting on Monday, and the man tells her she is lucky she didn't "end up in the hospital," so (C) and (D) are incorrect.

TIPS

• The man has lost his papers, but fortunately, the woman recalls seeing him carrying them to the parking garage. This reminds the man they are in his car. Therefore (A) and (B) are appropriate choices.

WARM-UP TRANSCRIPTS

1. (W) Who's the woman at the front desk? What happened to Amelie?
(M) Amelie's mother became very ill the day before yesterday, so she is taking some time off. She flew back to France this morning. We've had to bring in a temp until she gets back.
(W) I hope her mother is OK.

2. (M) I'd like to arrange for my rent to be paid by direct debit. I'm not sure which counter I should go to. Should I wait in that line of people over there?
(W) No, sir. All of the counters are just for transactions such as deposits, withdrawals, and payment of bills. To arrange a direct debit, you need the customer service desk. It's on the second floor.
(M) Oh, I see. Well, thank you very much. I'd better go on up then.

Question Type 3
Where Questions

Where questions mostly deal with a location, the position of something, or a place. Note, however, that the answer does not always include a preposition.

(Man)	Why did you miss the meeting on Monday morning? I thought you were supposed to give a report.
(Woman)	Well, I had a bad accident over the weekend, so I had to take my car to Charlie's garage to get it fixed. He doesn't open until 9:00 a.m., so I couldn't make it to the meeting.
(Man)	Gosh, I'm sorry to hear that. You're just lucky you didn't end up in the hospital getting fixed yourself.

i) Where did the woman go on Monday?

Correct answers:
(A) To Charlie's garage
(B) To see a mechanic

Incorrect answers:
(C) To the hospital
(D) To a meeting
(E) To an accident

(Man)	I can't find the handouts for the presentation that I'm supposed to make today. I made the copies just before I left to go home last night.
(Woman)	Well, you had a large pile of papers with you last night when I walked to the parking garage with you. Don't you remember? I had to open the door for you.
(Man)	Oh, yes. You're right. I put them in my car for safe keeping. I'll go get them now.

ii) Where is the man going?

Correct answers:
(A) To the parking garage
(B) To get papers from his car

Incorrect answers:
(C) To make a presentation
(D) To the copier room
(E) Home

Warm-ups

1. Where has Amelie gone?

   (A) To the front desk
   (C) To France

   (B) To a new job
   (D) To hospital

2. Where does the man need to go?

   (A) To the line of people waiting
   (C) To another branch of the bank

   (B) To the second floor
   (D) To the counter

Question Type 4
What Questions

PART 3

Short Conversations

Type 1 *Who* Questions
Type 2 *When* Questions
Type 3 *Where* Questions
Type 4 *What* Questions
Type 5 *How* Questions
Type 6 *Why* Questions
Type 7 *Which* Questions

What questions very often ask for detailed information about the content of a conversation. This information could be related to an object, idea, or action, or the information could be a description.

(Man) It's closing time. Why are you still working? Almost everyone else has left already.

(Woman) There's a big sale this weekend, and I've got to take inventory. I need to have an itemized list of everything in stock. I'm going to be here all night at this rate. It's taking much longer than I thought.

(Man) Why don't I help you with that? It'll be much quicker, and I have nothing planned for tonight.

TIPS

• The conversation mentions a "sale," so be careful not to confuse the word "sailing" in response (C). While (D) and (E) are true, they do not answer the question.

i) What is going on this weekend?

Correct answers:	Incorrect answers:
(A) There is a big sale at the store.	(C) The man and woman are going sailing.
(B) The store is having a sale.	(D) They will take the store's inventory.
	(E) The man will help the woman.

(Man) I can't seem to connect to the Internet today. Is anyone else having any trouble? It's really annoying because I need to send an urgent email to confirm an order.

(Woman) They are doing some maintenance work, and the server is down. If it's really that urgent, why don't you just confirm it by fax?

(Man) Yeah, I guess you're right. It would be better than nothing.

TIPS

• Responses (A) and (B) both refer to sending a fax, as is recommended by the woman. Responses (C) and (D) contain vocabulary mentioned in the conversation, but in both cases this is irrelevant.

ii) What does the woman suggest the man do?

Correct answers:	Incorrect answers:
(A) Send a fax	(C) Do some maintenance work
(B) Fax a confirmation of the order	(D) Confirm that the server is down

WARM-UP TRANSCRIPTS

1. (M) I'm looking for a flight to New York, leaving next Wednesday and returning the following Monday. I was wondering if you could let me know some air fares.
(W) Certainly. There's a round trip flight on Universal Airlines which costs $350 with tax, or there is a flight on National Airways for $320. Would you like to make a reservation for either of those flights?
(M) Not just yet. Let me call you back later.

Warm-ups

1. What does the man want?

   (A) To make a reservation

   (C) Information about air fares

   (B) A flight on Universal Airlines

   (D) A flight on National Airways

2. What does the woman decide?

   (A) To take a different color coat

   (C) To exchange the lining

   (B) To get a refund

   (D) To keep the coat just as it is

2. (W) Excuse me, I bought this coat here last week, but when I got it home I realized that there was a big rip in the lining. I'd like to exchange it for another.
(M) I'm sorry, but we don't have any more of that style in blue. Would you like to exchange it for a different color? We also have it in black and brown. Or we can give you a refund.
(W) Oh, well, no. I really like the blue. I'll just get my money back instead.

TIPS

• In the conversation, the man says that he has installed aromatherapy oil sprays, so any of responses (A) through (C) are appropriate.

TIPS

• Responses (A), (B), and (C) are appropriate choices because they all refer to the fact that the price of the monitors will be decreased. Response (D) is incorrect because the woman rejected the idea of gifts. Response (E) does not match the question type.

WARM-UP TRANSCRIPTS

1. (M) I have no idea how to use this fax machine. Have you ever used it? I can't work out which way up to put the paper.
   (W) Here, let me show you. First, you need to put the paper face down in the tray. Then dial the number you want. You'll know the fax was sent if you hear a long beep.
   (M) You make it look so easy.

2. (M) Simon has gone on vacation, but I really need to get his signature on this document before Thursday. Do you know where he went?
   (W) I'm not sure where he is, but he said that if anything urgent came up, we should call this number.
   (M) Great. I'll call him and get an address, then I can send him the document by courier service.

Answer Key
1 B 2 C

Question Type 5

How Questions

How questions often ask about the process, method or manner in which something is done, the quantity, or the quality of something. You should therefore pay careful attention to adjectives and adverbs.

(Man)   Have you noticed anything different? Don't you think the office seems much nicer lately?

(Woman)   Now that you mention it, I guess everyone seems a lot more relaxed and less easily upset. And I don't know what it is, but it seems to smell different than it used to.

(Man)   Right, I've installed aromatherapy oil sprays in each corner of the office. I use lemon oil in the morning for energy and lavender in the afternoon for relaxation.

i) How has the man improved the office environment?

Correct answers:

(A) By using aromatherapy oils
(B) By installing aromatherapy oil sprays
(C) With aromatherapy

Incorrect answers:

(D) By wearing lemon oil
(E) Because he is more relaxed

(Woman)   We have ordered too many of these monitors. They just aren't selling as well as we expected. I don't know how we are going to get rid of them.

(Man)   Why don't we put them on sale? Let's offer a 20% discount for two weeks and see if that helps. Or we could offer a free gift with them.

(Woman)   Let's try the discount. We don't have space to store any extra gifts at the moment.

ii) How are they going to try to improve sales of monitors?

Correct answers:

(A) By offering a discount
(B) By reducing the price
(C) By having a sale

Incorrect answers:

(D) By giving a free gift with each monitor
(E) Yes, they will improve sales.

Warm-ups

1. How will the man know if his fax was sent?

   (A) The woman will tell him.
   (B) He will hear a beeping noise.
   (C) He will not know.
   (D) He will put the paper face down.

2. How will the man get Simon's signature?

   (A) He'll send him a fax.
   (B) He cannot get the paper signed.
   (C) He'll call Simon, and then send the document.
   (D) He'll wait until Simon comes back.

Question Type 6

Why Questions

PART 3

Short Conversations

Type 1 *Who* Questions
Type 2 *When* Questions
Type 3 *Where* Questions
Type 4 *What* Questions
Type 5 *How* Questions
Type 6 *Why* Questions
Type 7 *Which* Questions

Why questions are concerned with a cause or reason. Questions of this type can often be in the negative. You may find it helpful to listen for words such as *because*, *since,* and *due to*.

(Man)   What are you doing with those boxes? You've been sorting through them for hours. Where did they come from?
(Woman)   These are from the storeroom. They are old accounting ledgers from the export office. I want to compare current profits with the profits we were making five years ago. It looks like things were a lot better then.
(Man)   Really? Let me have a look.

i) Why is the woman sorting through the boxes?

Correct answers:
(A) She wants to check company profits.
(B) She is comparing past and present profits.

Incorrect answers:
(C) They are from the storage room.
(D) The company was stronger in the past.

TIPS

- Responses (A) and (B) both answer "why" and give relevant information about the woman's reason for looking in the boxes. Response (C) does not answer "why", and (D) answers a different question.

(Woman)   Do you have any idea what has happened? The power is down, and nothing in the office is working. No one can get any work done.
(Man)   There was some kind of leak in the basement, and the generator short-circuited. They have been working on it since early this morning, but it seems to be more serious than they thought.
(Woman)   Well, I'm leaving. I'm going to work at home. I need electricity to use my computer, and some light would be nice.

ii) Why isn't the woman staying at the office?

Correct answers:
(A) Because there is a power outage.
(B) Because she can't work without electricity.

Incorrect answers:
(C) Because she quit her job.
(D) Because she started work early this morning.

TIPS

- In the conversation we learn that the office is suffering a power outage. Therefore, responses (A) and (B) are both appropriate choices. Responses (C) and (D) both contain information which is not mentioned in the conversation.

Warm-ups

1. Why is the shelf half empty?
   (A) The woman forgot to restock it.   (B) There are no dolls in the storeroom.
   (C) The dolls are selling rapidly.   (D) The man needs to restock it himself.

2. Why does Jim want to see the woman?
   (A) He wants to meet her for lunch.
   (B) He owes the woman some money.
   (C) He wants to discuss an idea.
   (D) He wants to call around three o'clock.

WARM-UP TRANSCRIPTS

1. (M) I asked you to restock this shelf with Happy Candy dolls about three hours ago, but it is still half empty. I don't want to have to ask you again.
   (W) I've restocked it twice, but we've already sold most of the dolls I put out. This is our most popular item at the moment. Everyone is buying these dolls for Christmas.
   (M) OK, then I'll call the storeroom and ask them to send up some more.

2. (M) Hey, can you go up to Jim's office? He asked me to send you up.
   (W) I wonder what he wants to talk to me about. I can't think of anything we need to discuss.
   (M) He said something about discussing a new idea for the advertising campaign. He doesn't like the current one.

Answer Key 1 C 2 C

43

TIPS

- After considering the advantages of the brown desk, the man says that is the desk he will order. We also learn that the brown desk has three drawers, making both (A) and (B) possible responses.

TIPS

- The woman wants someone efficient and reliable. From the man's description, we learn that Kenichi is the least able to do the job; therefore, only responses (A) and (B) are appropriate here.

WARM-UP TRANSCRIPTS

1. (M) I'm entertaining an important client and his wife next week. I have no idea where to go. Last time, I took them to a classical concert, but they didn't seem to enjoy it much.
(W) I'd go to a musical. How about *The Life of Mozart?* That's popular, or there's *Happy Days.*
(M) *The Life of Mozart* sounds too classical for their tastes. Guess we'll be seeing *Happy Days.*

2. (W) My long distance provider charges far too much. I'm using PST, but I need to change. Can you recommend anyone to me? What company do you use?
(M) I just changed from All Teleco to Tele Express. They only charge 10 cents a minute.
(W) Well, that's even more than I pay. I'll just have to stick with PST.

Question Type 7
Which Questions

Which questions ask about alternative choices. It is not possible to answer these questions using *yes* or *no*. You may find it helpful to listen for the conjunction *or* in the conversation to alert you to alternatives which may be relevant for choosing the correct response.

(Man) I've been thinking of getting a new desk, and I've narrowed it down to these two in this catalog. They are both about the same size and price, so it's hard to choose between them.
(Woman) I like the three drawers in the brown one. The gray desk only has two. Also, the brown one has a nice built-in pen holder, and the legs look a lot sturdier, don't they?
(Man) Well, I think you've made up my mind for me. That's the one I'll order.

i) Which desk is the man going to buy?

Correct answers:
(A) The brown one
(B) The desk with three drawers

Incorrect answers:
(C) The gray desk
(D) He cannot decide.

(Woman) Who do you think is more reliable, Hirotaka, Asako, or Kenichi? I need someone I can really rely on to help me with the next shipment.
(Man) I've never had problems with any of them. But I know that Mr. Ito in accounts has complained that Kenichi is not very good at tracking down payments from clients. He also tends to be late submitting paperwork, but he always does it very thoroughly.
(Woman) I need someone who can get things done on time. I guess I know who not to choose.

ii) Which employee is the woman NOT going to choose?

Correct answers:
(A) Kenichi
(B) The employee who submits work late

Incorrect answers:
(C) Hirotaka
(D) Asako
(E) Hirotaka or Asako

Warm-ups

1. Which musical will the man take his clients to?
   (A) *Happy Days*
   (B) Neither, they sound awful.
   (C) *The Life of Mozart*
   (D) He'll probably take them to a classical concert.

2. Which long distance provider does the woman think is best for her?
   (A) Tele Express
   (B) Her current provider
   (C) All Teleco
   (D) It isn't mentioned.

Sample Test: PART 3

Choose the best answer to each question.

1. What has the man already done?
   (A) Distributed materials
   (B) Sorted names
   (C) Prepared address labels
   (D) Made photocopies

2. Who will prepare the labels?
   (A) The woman
   (B) The man and the woman
   (C) The man
   (D) The secretary

3. When will the labels be ready?
   (A) Tomorrow afternoon
   (B) Before lunch time
   (C) By the end of the day
   (D) Around 2:00 in the afternoon

---

4. Why did the man place a newspaper advertisement?
   (A) He is looking for a new manager.
   (B) He is trying to sell something.
   (C) He is looking for a new job.
   (D) The woman asked him to.

5. The last manager was probably what kind of person?
   (A) Easy to get along with
   (B) Relaxed
   (C) Hardworking
   (D) Tense and difficult to get along with

6. What is the man going to do?
   (A) Place an ad in the newspaper
   (B) Look at the résumés
   (C) Keep his promises
   (D) Talk to the new manager

7. Where are the speakers?
   (A) In a department store
   (B) In a supermarket
   (C) At an airport
   (D) At a post office

8. Which bag will the man check?
   (A) The black suitcase
   (B) He'll only carry his computer.
   (C) His green bag
   (D) The green bag and the black suitcase

9. How many items will the man carry on to the plane?
   (A) One
   (B) Two
   (C) Three
   (D) Four

---

10. When did the woman join the company?
    (A) A few years ago
    (B) Next week
    (C) Yesterday
    (D) Two years ago

11. Who is the woman?
    (A) A new manager
    (B) A doctor
    (C) The new fund manager
    (D) The new accountant

12. What is the woman going to do?
    (A) Have lunch with Ben Reilly
    (B) Meet the rest of the staff
    (C) Talk to the manager
    (D) Make an announcement

13. What is the man working on?

   (A) The August vacation schedule
   (B) A price list for the sales
   (C) The August sales report
   (D) A questionnaire

14. When does the man have to submit the sales report?

   (A) Tomorrow morning
   (B) Today, before he goes home
   (C) By August
   (D) Tomorrow afternoon

15. Why does the man have to finish his work today?

   (A) The computers won't be working tomorrow.
   (B) The woman needs to read his report.
   (C) He is taking a vacation tomorrow.
   (D) He is going on a business trip tomorrow.

---

16. Where is this conversation probably taking place?

   (A) In a hotel
   (B) In a post office
   (C) In a hospital
   (D) In a school

17. What must the woman do?

   (A) Order a meal
   (B) Write a check
   (C) Deliver a box
   (D) Fill out a form

18. When will the packages arrive?

   (A) In a few hours
   (B) Sometime tomorrow
   (C) Later today
   (D) Probably next week

19. What is the problem?

   (A) The printer has run out of ink.
   (B) The printer is getting too old.
   (C) The woman has lost a file.
   (D) The man has broken the printer.

20. When did the printer last break down?

   (A) Tuesday
   (B) Three times this week
   (C) Wednesday
   (D) Monday

21. What do the two people think their company should do?

   (A) Buy a new printer
   (B) Replace the repairman
   (C) Increase the printing budget
   (D) Make more repairs

---

22. How many jobs is the woman considering?

   (A) Two
   (B) Five
   (C) One
   (D) Three

23. What are the disadvantages of the first position?

   (A) It offers vacations and the chance to travel.
   (B) It is only for one month.
   (C) It doesn't look interesting.
   (D) It doesn't pay very well.

24. Which position will the woman apply for?

   (A) Personnel manager
   (B) Neither position
   (C) Personal assistant
   (D) Professor

25. How did the woman try to contact the man?

(A) By fax
(B) With the budget
(C) By phone and email
(D) By Monday

26. What does the woman ask the man to do?

(A) Finish a project this weekend
(B) Begin making a budget
(C) Take the weekend off
(D) Work on the budget

28. Why might the company be going out of business?

(A) Because of employee rumors
(B) Due to poor sales
(C) Because of slow business
(D) Due to higher manufacturing costs

29. Why does the man think the company is in a stable condition?

(A) Sales are strong.
(B) He likes his job.
(C) It's the biggest in town.
(D) It's nonsense.

30. What is happening?

(A) Employees are unhappy.
(B) People are quitting.
(C) The company is losing money.
(D) The woman wants a new job.

Transcripts: PART 3

Questions 1 through 3 refer to the following conversation.

(M) These files have been photocopied and are ready to be distributed. All we need to do now is put them in the envelopes and label them. There's a big box of A4 envelopes in the storeroom.

(W) Did you prepare the address labels yet? I know that you said you were going to take charge of that.

(M) Not yet. I have to sort the names, but it won't take me long. They should be ready before lunch. We'll be able to mail them this afternoon.

Questions 4 through 6 refer to the following conversation.

(M) I posted that newspaper ad for the new manager's position just three days ago, and I've already gotten twenty résumés. That's more than I was expecting.

(W) How do they look? Are there any that look promising? I hope you'll find someone a lot more easy-going and relaxed than the last manager you hired.

(M) Well, I haven't read them yet. I'm planning on doing that this afternoon.

(W) Better you than me.

Questions 7 through 9 refer to the following conversation.

(W) Sir, I'm afraid that I'm going to have to ask you to check-in one of your bags, please. New policies allow only one carry-on on domestic flights.

(M) Oh, well if it's absolutely necessary. This one has all the documents I need to read on the flight, so I'll check the black suitcase.

(W) Thank you. You can take the green bag and your laptop computer as carry on baggage.

Questions 10 through 12 refer to the following conversation.

(M) Excuse me, but you don't look familiar. I don't think I've seen you before. Are you new here?

(W) Yes, I am. I'm the new accountant. Yesterday was my first day. I'll be meeting the rest of the staff this afternoon. I'm feeling a little nervous.

(M) Well, it's nice to meet you. I'm Ben Reilly. I've been here for two years, and don't worry, everyone is easy to get along with.

(W) That's good to hear.

Questions 13 through 15 refer to the following conversation.

(W) How are you doing, Jake? You look really busy.

(M) I need to submit the August sales report by tomorrow afternoon. I've nearly finished, but there are still a couple of pages to write. Perhaps I'll just finish it off tomorrow morning. I'm getting kind of tired.

(W) Um, you know, you might want to take care of it today, since the computers will be down tomorrow.

(M) I forgot about that. I'm glad you reminded me. I'd better finish before I head home.

Questions 16 through 18 refer to the following conversation.

(M) Good afternoon. What can I do for you?

(W) I'd like to send this letter by standard mail. Then, I need to send these packages. They are part of a rush order, so I need them to arrive as soon as possible. What's the fastest way to mail them?

(M) I'd recommend priority delivery. Here, fill out this order form and check the "priority delivery" box. The packages should arrive sometime tomorrow.

Questions 19 through 21 refer to the following conversation.

(W) Oh, no. The printer isn't working again. The paper is going through, but there is nothing on it. And I put in a new ink cartridge yesterday.

(M) It's the third time this week. It wouldn't work properly Monday, Tuesday, or Wednesday either. Why don't they replace that piece of junk? It's just getting too old.

(W) Exactly. With all the money the company spends repairing it, they could buy three new ones.

(M) You try telling that to the management.

Questions 22 through 24 refer to the following conversation.

(W) I can't decide between these two jobs. They both look pretty interesting. One is for a personal assistant. The salary is not great, but they offer five weeks vacation and travel opportunities. The other is for a personnel manager. It pays more, but offers only two weeks off a year.

(M) Well, do you want time or money? It seems pretty simple to me.

(W) Well, I'd really rather have time to relax. Money isn't everything. I'll try for the personal assistant position.

Questions 25 through 27 refer to the following conversation.

(W) I've been trying to contact you for ages. You never seem to answer your phone or check your email. Did you finish the budget projections?

(M) Not quite. I've finished the bulk of the work, so they'll probably be ready by the middle of next week.

(W) Don't forget that Mr. Rogers needs some preliminary figures by Monday morning to present at the meeting in the afternoon. Get them done this weekend, all right?

(M) OK. I guess I'll be spending the weekend at the office.

Questions 28 through 30 refer to the following conversation.

(W) I've heard a rumor that we might be going out of business. Is it true? Do you know anything about it? Are we going to lose our jobs?

(M) That's nonsense. Sales have been increasing for months now. No one is going to be laid off if sales are going up.

(W) Yes, but operating costs have been going up even faster. I've heard that the company hasn't broken even for months. We're running at a loss.

(M) Gosh, I really had no idea.

4 | Short Talks

Strategies

This section of the TOEIC® includes short talks given by one speaker, usually in the form of a news or business report, commercial or public service advertisement, recorded phone message, or public announcement, followed by questions about the talks. While you're listening, you should keep looking at the questions, which will enable you to focus your listening on specific information. The questions typically ask about the main idea, details, or inferences.

Test-taking Tips

✓ Do not be misled by your general knowledge; you should only use the information given in the talk.

✓ In general, the questions are organized in the order in which the information is given in the talk, so try to answer the question while listening to the talk.

✓ Before you hear the statements, read as many questions as you can.

Question Types

Type 1 — Main Idea Questions
Type 2 — Fact and Detail Questions
Type 3 — Inference Questions
Type 4 — Cause and Effect Questions

PART 4
Short Talks
Type 1 Main Idea Questions
Type 2 Fact and Detail Questions
Type 3 Inference Questions
Type 4 Cause and Effect Questions

Question Type 1
Main Idea Questions

Look for key words or phrases that will help you figure out the main topic of the talk. Try to focus on things such as the purpose of the talk and the general theme of the talk. Obviously, the main idea will vary widely from talk to talk.

Main idea questions often take the following forms:
- After a talk advertising a slimming aid — *What is this commercial about?*
  Possible answer: *A product for losing weight*
- After a traffic report talking about delays and traffic jams — *What happened?*
  Possible answer: *There was a traffic accident.*
- After a public service type announcement — *What is the purpose of the message?*
  Possible answer: *To warn people about pickpockets on the subway system*

KEY EXPRESSIONS

- **lately** — recently
- **the answer to your needs** — providing you with essentials
- **under one roof** — in one location

Key Information

1, 2, 4

The talk is describing one large store that sells groceries.

3

This gives us information about the event being advertised

Questions 1 through 3 refer to the following advertisement.

W: You may have already heard of Jesters, but have you paid us a visit lately? We are the local answer to all your ¹**food shopping needs.** We have everything you could want, ²**all under one roof.** We closed recently due to a large fire, but now we're back with a ³**grand reopening sale** in our new location. To celebrate our first week back in business, we are offering discounts of up to 50% on all of our most popular grocery lines. At our in-store bakery, we're even offering a free birthday cake to everyone who has a birthday this week.

Jesters — you know us. ⁴**We're the store** where everyone goes home laughing thanks to our everyday savings on the brands you love. Come find us on the Bluewater Interstate just north of Fayetteville.

1. What is being advertised?
   - (A) A supermarket
   - (B) The Bluewater Interstate
   - (C) Birthday cakes
   - (D) Groceries

2. What is the purpose of this talk?
   - (A) To talk about new products
   - (B) To inform customers that the store has reopened
   - (C) To offer special discounts
   - (D) To introduce the in-store bakery

3. Why was the store closed?
   - (A) It wasn't popular.
   - (B) The building was sold.
   - (C) It was damaged in a fire.
   - (D) They didn't have enough staff.

Question Type 2
Fact and Detail Questions

PART 4

Short Talks

Type 1   Main Idea Questions

Type 2   Fact and Detail Questions

Type 3   Inference Questions

Type 4   Cause and Effect Questions

For this type of question, you will need to focus on precise facts and details. Therefore, look for key words or phrases such as numbers, times, descriptions of a situation, and other words that will help you figure out the specific details of the short talk.

Detail questions often take the following forms:
- After a talk including the following sentence: "There will be heavy rainfall for most of the day."
  — *What will the weather be like?* Possible answer: *It will rain all day.*
- After a talk including the following sentence: "The flight lands at 3:30, so we expect them to arrive here about 2 hours later."
  — *What time will they arrive?* Possible answer: *At around 5:30*
- After a talk including the following sentence: "Medimind's handy alarm can be set to help you remember to take your medication."
  — *What is the product?* Possible answer: *An alarm to remind people to take medicine*

Questions 1 through 3 refer to the following weather report.

M: This is Dusty White coming to you live from the Weather Station here in [1]**Victorville.** The mild temperatures we have been enjoying in recent days are finally over. Brace yourself for a [2]**big drop in temperature.** The [3]**highs today will be around 32 degrees** with tonight's [4]**lows dropping to near zero,** and a [5]**wind chill of more than 20 below.** Winter weather is coming on very quickly this year as we are [6]**expecting our first major snowfall by tomorrow afternoon.** A major storm moving slowly across the plains has already brought five feet of snow to some areas not too far west of here. [7]**Locally, we are projecting anywhere from three to five feet of snow in the next 48-72 hours.** My advice is to bundle up and bring in the animals. Stay warm and keep on watching your favorite weather channel.

1. What will today's highest temperature be?
   (A) Around -20 degrees   (B) From three to five degrees
   (C) Around 32 degrees   (D) From 48 to 72 degrees

2. What advice does the reporter give?
   (A) Enjoy the snow   (B) Bring your animals inside
   (C) Keep your radio on   (D) Change the channel

3. How much snow does the reporter expect in this area?
   (A) Three to five feet   (B) Close to zero
   (C) 48 to 72 feet   (D) 20 feet

KEY EXPRESSIONS
- **brace yourself** — prepare yourself for something bad or severe
- **wind chill** — the effect that wind has on how cold the air feels
- **bundle up** — wear enough to keep warm

Key Information

[1]
The speaker's location

[2]
The weather will change suddenly.

[3,4]
The highest temperature will be 32 degrees/the lowest around zero.

[5,6]
Heavy snow is expected.

[7]
People should stay indoors.

PART 4
Short Talks

Type 1   Main Idea Questions
Type 2   Fact and Detail Questions
Type 3   Inference Questions
Type 4   Cause and Effect Questions

Question Type 3

Inference Questions

Inference questions check your ability to draw a conclusion based on the facts and details that are provided in the short talk. Although the answer is not stated explicitly in the talk, it will provide you with enough information to choose the correct answer. As in main idea questions and detail questions, you should look for key words or phrases that will help you to choose the correct answer by drawing a logical conclusion.

Inference questions and their answers often take some of the following forms:
- After a talk including the following sentence: "She doesn't live in the apartment any more."
  - *Where did the woman used to live?* Possible answer: *In an apartment*
- After a talk including the following sentence: "Rarely do I pass the tennis court and not see him out there playing."
  - *How often does the man play tennis?* Possible answer: *He plays frequently.*

KEY EXPRESSIONS

- **retroactive** — taking effect from a date in the past
- **debit card** — a kind of ATM card

Key Information

1, 2

These words are clues to Cindy's line of work.

2

The insurance takes effect from the date of application.

3

The company does not really want clients to pay directly at the office.

4

Cindy is going to provide additional information to the customer later.

Questions 1 through 3 refer to the following phone message.

W: Mr. Blanchard, this is Cindy Gerber at Capital ¹**Coverage.** Well, I've got some answers to a couple of your questions, but not all of them. First of all, your ²**insurance is retroactive to the day you applied for it,** so your foot injury is covered. Second, yes, ³**you may make your payments at our office, though we prefer that you mail them in.** If you do pay us directly, you must do so by check or credit card. We don't take cash or debit cards here. ⁴**As for your other inquiries, I'll have to do some checking, so I will get back to you** as soon as I can. Please don't hesitate to call me during office hours if you have questions about any of this information. Or, you can leave a recorded message after 6:00 p.m. Take care.

1. Where does Cindy Gerber work?
   (A) At a public information desk   (B) At an insurance agency
   (C) At a credit card company   (D) At the telephone company

2. What has Mr. Blanchard previously inquired about?
   (A) How he may pay his bill   (B) What to put on his injury
   (C) Where Cindy Gerber works   (D) When he will be called back

3. What time does the office probably close?
   (A) Only on weekends   (B) About 5:00 p.m.
   (C) 6:00 p.m.   (D) During office hours

Question Type 4
Cause and Effect Questions

PART 4

Short Talks

Type 1   Main Idea Questions

Type 2   Fact and Detail Questions

Type 3   Inference Questions

Type 4   Cause and Effect Questions

Cause and effect questions look at either an event or an action, and either the reason for it happening (the cause), or the consequences which it has already had or might have in the future (effect). For this type of question, you may find it helpful to listen for expressions such as *because (of), due to, owing to, as a result of,* and *thanks to* in order to focus on cause. However, these expressions may not always be used.

Cause and effect questions often take the following forms:
- After a talk including the following sentence: "There is heavy traffic on Highway 32 owing to a ten-car pile up."
  — *Why is traffic heavy on the highway?* Possible answer: *Because of a car accident*
- After a talk including the following sentence: "Hurricane Michael is expected to hit the coast of Florida later this evening. There is a high possibility of flooding."
  — *What may happen because of the hurricane?* Possible answer: *Floods*

Questions 1 through 3 refer to the following traffic report.

M: Good evening. You are listening to Radio F1. Those of you headed into Liversmead on [1]**Highway 2** are in for some long delays. [2]**Owing to a collision between an oil tanker and a bus, traffic is backed up to the Silverbridge Intersection.** Emergency vehicles are at the scene, but due to the [3]**flammable nature of the oil, they are proceeding very slowly. It is expected to take about 5 hours to safely clear up the area.** The accident occurred at 4:30 this morning when the [4]**driver of the tanker dropped her cell phone. She looked down to pick it up and inadvertently veered into the opposite lane.** Luckily, the bus had no passengers. Neither driver was injured. You might want to call the office and let them know you'll be late. Hands-free, of course. We don't want any more accidents.

1. What has caused delays on Highway 2?

    (A) Animals on the road   (B) A collision between a car and a tanker
    (C) A broken traffic light   (D) An accident involving a bus

2. Why is it taking so long to clear up the accident?

    (A) There is a danger of fire.   (B) There are no emergency vehicles available.
    (C) The road is slippery.   (D) It is too dark.

3. How did the accident happen?

    (A) A bus overturned.   (B) The tanker driver was distracted by her cell phone.
    (C) The cars skidded on ice.   (D) The vehicles were speeding.

KEY EXPRESSIONS

- **at the scene** — at the location
- **flammable** — easy to burn

Key Information

[1]
Gives the location of the incident

[2]
Explains the current situation

[3]
Provides details and possible problems

[4]
Tells how the incident occurred

Sample Test: PART 4

Choose the best answer to each question.

1. What does the speaker do for a living?
   (A) She is a scientist who studies weather conditions.
   (B) She is a weather reporter.
   (C) She is unemployed.
   (D) She is responsible for organizing Dartmoor.

2. How long has the speaker been measuring precipitation?
   (A) All day
   (B) For about 5 years
   (C) Since childhood
   (D) From yesterday morning

3. What is a possible consequence of some of the change she is noticing?
   (A) Cooler temperatures
   (B) Droughts
   (C) Flooding
   (D) Rainfall

4. Why did the speaker take up yoga?
   (A) He was interested in a career change.
   (B) He wanted to avoid injury.
   (C) He was interested in meditation.
   (D) He had always wanted to learn yoga.

5. What was causing the speaker's injuries?
   (A) Excessive soccer practice
   (B) Contorted positions
   (C) A lack of practice last season
   (D) Stress

6. What benefits has yoga given him?
   (A) It has given him greater flexibility and better stress management.
   (B) It has given him greater flexibility and made him thinner.
   (C) It has mentally drained him and given him more flexible muscles.
   (D) It has helped him become a personal trainer.

7. What is the purpose of this talk?
   (A) To recruit consultants with a knowledge of a foreign language
   (B) To promote overseas investment
   (C) To find new clients hoping to invest overseas
   (D) To talk about the benefits of knowing a second language

8. What does the man's company do?
   (A) Arrange tours in the Middle East and Asia
   (B) Liaise between American companies and overseas companies
   (C) Produce books on business etiquette
   (D) Develop special tours for business travelers

9. What kind of person do you probably need to be to work for this company?
   (A) Adventurous and outgoing
   (B) Diplomatic and flexible
   (C) Changeable and aggressive
   (D) Reserved and flexible

10. What is the topic of this talk?
    (A) The convenience of travel these days
    (B) The consequences of tourism
    (C) The beaches of the Mediterranean
    (D) The ruins of Petra

11. How many examples does the speaker give to support her argument?
    (A) 1
    (B) 2
    (C) 3
    (D) 4

12. Which of the following is NOT mentioned as being damaged by tourism?
    (A) The ruins of Petra
    (B) The Mediterranean sea
    (C) The Pyramids
    (D) The Alps

13. What is the purpose of the speaker's speech?
    (A) To announce his retirement and name his replacement
    (B) To reminisce about his life
    (C) To talk about his grandchildren
    (D) To ask people to make a donation to Margaret Withers

14. How long has the speaker been the town council chairperson?
    (A) 10 years
    (B) A decade
    (C) 20 years
    (D) Less than a year

15. How many members are there on the town council?
    (A) 11
    (B) 12
    (C) 13
    (D) We do not know.

16. What is the purpose of this announcement?
    (A) To inform passengers of their flight number
    (B) To inform passengers of a cancellation
    (C) To inform passengers of a delay
    (D) To inform passengers of an accident

17. Who should report to the ticket counter?
    (A) All flight FE303 passengers
    (B) All passengers traveling to New York
    (C) All flight FE303 passengers whose final destination is New York
    (D) All flight FE303 passengers transferring to other flights in New York

18. Who may use the VIP lounge on this occasion?
    (A) All Foreign Airlines passengers
    (B) All flight FE303 passengers
    (C) Only VIPs on the flight
    (D) All visitors to the airport

19. What can be said about Albertus Grimvich?

    (A) He produces about three movies every year.
    (B) He is not very successful.
    (C) He sacrifices quality for quantity.
    (D) He is not very well known.

20. What is true about Albertus Grimvich's career?

    (A) He used to be a company director.
    (B) He used to struggle to find financial backing.
    (C) He used to be a door-to-door salesman.
    (D) It does not say.

21. Which of the following statements is NOT true?

    (A) Critics generally do not like Albertus Grimvich's movies.
    (B) Albertus Grimvich is from Albania.
    (C) Albertus Grimvich released three films in 2005.
    (D) Albertus Grimvich's rise to fame was fast.

22. Who is the speaker probably talking to?

    (A) Politicians
    (B) High school students
    (C) Home makers
    (D) University students

23. What is the purpose of this speech?

    (A) To ask people to vote for her
    (B) To encourage young people to vote
    (C) To complain about her job
    (D) To discuss politics in other countries

24. How did the speaker become president?

    (A) She wanted to be president.
    (B) She probably paid a lot of money.
    (C) People voted for her.
    (D) She used her vote in her mid-twenties.

25. What can be inferred about the speaker?

    (A) He is a movie star.
    (B) He is a retired stockbroker.
    (C) He is a writer.
    (D) He is an investment banker.

26. What three things made the speaker successful?

    (A) Eavesdropping, investments, and money
    (B) Hard work, resolve, and chance
    (C) Reading the right books, luck, and hard work
    (D) Effort, talent, and luck

27. What does the speaker believe about luck?

    (A) Luck is not easy to find.
    (B) Talented people don't need luck.
    (C) Everyone needs a little luck.
    (D) Luck is dumb.

28. Who is the presentation probably aimed at?

    (A) Computer programmers
    (B) Businesses wanting to improve their computer security
    (C) Businesses interested in science
    (D) Businesses related to national security

29. Why is cryptography important for businesses?

    (A) They need it to ensure transactions are secure.
    (B) They need to be able to send secret messages to other companies.
    (C) It is not important for businesses because they can use the Internet instead.
    (D) It can protect national security.

30. Which of the following statements is NOT correct?

    (A) The speaker expects everyone to already know about cryptography.
    (B) Cryptography is the art of secret communication.
    (C) Cryptography used to be used mainly for national and military security.
    (D) Cryptography is growing in importance in the 21st century.

Transcripts: PART 4

Questions 1 through 3 refer to the following talk.

(W) I have always been interested in the environment. When I was a child, I used to collect rain water in the garden and measure how much it had rained. I even used to make charts of how much rain I had collected. I doubt that my measurements were very accurate, but I used to enjoy it. I still measure rainfall. However, nowadays I get paid for it because I work as a meteorologist for an environmental organization. I am responsible for analyzing precipitation in the Dartmoor region of the United Kingdom. I analyze average monthly rainfall and compare this to the previous year's rainfall. I have been seeing an overall drop in average precipitation over the last five years. Although the reduction is currently very slight, it is significant and could lead to a serious drought over time. I believe that people should be made aware of this kind of environmental change.

Questions 4 through 6 refer to the following talk.

(M) As a professional soccer player, it is essential for me to keep my body in tip top condition. However, last season I found that I was getting a lot of injuries which, although not serious, were preventing me from playing my best. Several months ago, my personal trainer suggested taking up yoga. At first, I really wasn't keen on the idea because I had images of lots of people in contorted positions, and I didn't see how it would help me avoid injury. Anyway, I gave it a try, and it immediately improved my game. My muscles are much more flexible, and more surprisingly, it has helped me deal with the stresses of a professional match. I have realized that a lot of my injuries were a result of stress. Soccer is mentally and physically draining. The meditation techniques I am learning in yoga help me calm down after a game, instead of feeling stressed and burnt out.

Questions 7 through 9 refer to the following talk.

(M) I have been working as a consultant for over twenty years, providing assistance to companies who find themselves doing business in countries where they have no knowledge or understanding of the language or culture. As more and more countries have become open to overseas investors, this need has increased. Despite political tensions in Asia and the Middle East, I am receiving an overwhelming number of requests for briefings on the cultural and business etiquette in the various countries in these regions. For this reason, I am looking to expand my team of experts. Of course, while I do not want to have to turn away potential clients, it is of the utmost importance that all our consultants, whether they are based in the United States, or are based in-country with the client, must be completely fluent in the language of the country they choose to represent. They must also be able to deal with the difficult challenges of liaising between the client and their intended business interest. Travel is a common feature of this job, often at the last minute, and more often than not the reality does not match the glamorous image of an airline advertisement. If you feel you are up to the job, application packages are available at the back of the room.

Questions 10 through 12 refer to the following talk.

(W) We take it for granted these days that we have the right to go just about anywhere we want to in the world. If there is an airplane, or a boat, or someone we can pay to take us, then we will go there, no matter how far or remote the place is. However, have you ever stopped to think how harmful this is to the places we visit? Well, it is harmful. Tourism is destroying many of the beautiful places so many of us dream of visiting. Let me give you some examples. Did you know that the beaches of the Mediterranean have over 100 million visitors every year, but that all these visitors have made the Mediterranean the dirtiest sea in the world? Shocking, isn't it? And the ruins of Petra in Jordan are in danger of being destroyed by the thousands of tourists that go there every day! The ruins are made of a soft stone, eroded by the footsteps of each visitor. Even hiking in the Alps can cause damage to the delicate ecosystem of the mountains, killing flora and fauna. So before you set out to see the wonders of the world, ask yourself, "Is it really worth it?"

Questions 13 through 15 refer to the following speech.

(M) When I was first invited to become the chairperson of the Greenport town council, I rather doubted my own ability to do justice to the position. Little did I imagine that I would hold the position for two whole decades. However, I feel that it is now time to hand the post over to someone younger, and I don't think we could have made a better choice. I am certain that Margaret Withers, who has lived in Greenport all her life, will do a very good job as the new chairperson. She was chosen in what was the first ever unanimous decision by the town council. Let's hope that this is a sign that she will help maintain peace and harmony among the eleven other members of the council. I myself will be withdrawing completely from local politics in order to spend more time working on my long-neglected garden and playing with my grandchildren. Margaret, I wish you the very best of luck, and congratulations on your new post. I hope you enjoy it as much as I did.

Questions 16 through 18 refer to the following announcement.

(W) Attention please, attention. All passengers for flight FE303 bound for New York, due to depart at 13:35, we regret to inform you of a change to this flight. Due to security reasons, this flight will no longer be departing at 13:35. Please listen for further announcements regarding the new departure time. We are very sorry for the inconvenience this may cause passengers. A new gate number for boarding will be posted as soon as we are able to confirm departure time. Again, for security reasons, flight FE303 will be delayed until further notice. Any passengers who are scheduled to take transfer flights upon arrival in New York, please make your way to the Foreign Eastern Airlines ticket counter located in the arrivals lounge on the first floor. They will be able to assist you in making arrangements in the event that you will be unable to make your connecting flight. In the meantime, Foreign Eastern Airlines invites all boarding pass holders for flight FE303 to visit the VIP lounge where we will be serving a variety of cold drinks and snacks to passengers.

Questions 19 through 21 refer to the following talk.

(M) International box office figures for 2005 have just been released, and yet again one director stands out above all the others. Albertus Grimvich is one of the most prolific directors of our times, but in his case, quantity certainly doesn't seem to harm quality. Although he released a total of three movies last year, as in the preceding three years, all of them were both critical and box office successes. What I think is most remarkable is the rapid success of this Albanian film director. Just a few years ago he confessed to knocking on his neighbors' doors begging for money to develop his projects. Nowadays, of course, major businesses knock on his door, asking to be allowed to sponsor his films, knowing that being associated with any work of his will bring great financial benefits. With this kind of backing, it is no wonder that he is able to produce such great movies.

Questions 22 through 24 refer to the following speech.

(W) Although I am the first female president of this nation, you might be surprised to know that I wasn't at all interested in politics when I was younger. Just like many of you here today, when I too was a university student, I thought that politicians were just a bunch of old men doing things to please themselves, not to serve the people. I'm ashamed to say I didn't even use my vote until I was in my mid-twenties. I regret that now, and I want to make sure that you don't make the same mistake. Hundreds and hundreds of people all over the world have lost, and continue to lose their lives in order to secure the right to vote in fair elections in their countries. But here in our country, thousands of people just ignore their own right to vote. Then those same people will turn around and complain about their local politicians, they complain about the government. Well, I'm not president just because I want to be. I'm here because some people voted for me. If you don't like this government, you are the only ones with the power to make a change. And you know how to do that, don't you?

Answer Key

1 C	2 A	29 A	30 A
3 B	4 B	27 C	28 B
5 A	6 D	25 B	26 B
7 B	8 A	23 B	24 C
9 B	10 B	21 A	22 D
11 C	12 C	19 A	20 B
13 C	14 A	17 D	18 B
15 C	16 B		

61

<u>**Questions 25 through 27**</u> refer to the following report.

(M) I am often asked about the secret of my success, and I have to reply that, well, there is no secret. Investments are not hidden, and anyone can make them. I'm not sure exactly what you want me to say when you ask me, "So what's your secret, John?" The biographies and autobiographies of numerous successful people are out there for everyone to read, as is my own autobiography which was published after my retirement last year. All I can say for sure is that I got where I am today through my own hard work, determination, and a little luck. I do believe that no matter how much talent a person may have and no matter how hard he or she works, it is likely to come to nothing without a little bit of dumb luck. It might be something as simple as being in the right place at the right time, reading the right newspaper article and spotting an investment opportunity. My first lucky break came as a result of a conversation I overheard. While two of my rivals were busy arguing over who was going to make the pitch for their new concept, I noted down some of the names they mentioned and went directly to the people myself. Then I presented my own ideas, beating them to it.

<u>**Questions 28 through 30**</u> refer to the following talk.

(W) In today's lecture, I'd like to focus your attention on cryptography. I know that this is something that most of you may not be familiar with, but chances are it is already used at some level within your own business. Cryptography is, quite simply, the art of secret communication. You may think this sounds rather old fashioned, but it is in fact of greater and greater relevance in the 21st century. It used to be something used mainly for military purposes and national security. But nowadays it is important for protecting the privacy of individuals. I mean this in terms of online business transactions, e-banking, and any time you need to transfer personal information through a computer. We all maintain large databases of customer details, of our own transactions, and in fact everything is stored in a computer somewhere. Strong cryptography is required in order to guarantee security every time a transaction is made online in a world where e-commerce is becoming more common. Using a cryptograph, which is, of course, not viewable by the computer user, information is scrambled so that it can pass to its destination unseen by others. This is especially important to protect credit card and bank account numbers, or to prevent the leakage of secret information.

The TOEIC®
Reading Section

The Reading Comprehension Section of the TOEIC® consists of three parts: Incomplete Sentences, Incomplete Texts, and Reading Comprehension. There are a total of one hundred questions. All the information necessary to answer the questions is printed in your text booklet. You will have seventy-five minutes to complete the entire Reading Section of the exam. You may divide the time between the sections in any manner you choose.

Part 5	Incomplete Sentences	40 questions
Part 6	Incomplete Texts	12 questions
Part 7	Reading Comprehension	48 questions

| Reading Total | | 100 questions |

5 Incomplete Sentences

Strategies

This section of the TOEIC® typically checks the scope of your vocabulary knowledge, along with your ability to make correct use of words and phrases. When choosing the answer, you should pay close attention to grammatical points such as parts of speech, tenses, agreement, positions of frequency adverbs, etc. Note also that the words around the missing word can be useful clues for the answer. Pay close attention to the type of word you are asked to find. If the question asks you to find a noun, look only for nouns; disregard any verbs, adverbs, adjectives, etc. in the selection list.

Test-taking Tips

✓ Determine whether the question is about vocabulary or about grammar.

✓ If it is a vocabulary question, think of the meaning of the whole sentence.

✓ If it is a grammar question, determine the part of speech needed for the blank by taking a close look at the surrounding elements.

✓ Remember that quite a lot of English words look and sound similar, sometimes even the same, even though the meaning is different.

Question Types

Type 1 — Vocabulary Questions
- Verbs
- Nouns
- Modifiers
- Conjunctions
- Prepositions

Type 2 — Grammar Questions
- Verbs
- Auxiliary Verbs
- Subject-verb Agreement
- Gerunds and Infinitives
- Nouns and Pronouns
- Conjunctions
- Comparatives and Superlatives
- Negation

Question Type 1

Vocabulary Questions

Verbs

Though verbs and nouns are different classes of words, sometimes they may look or sound similar, for example, the verb *present,* which means to give, and the noun *present,* which means a gift. Sometimes a verb and a noun may look or sound exactly the same, as in the case of *ride. Ride* is a verb which means to get in or on a large vehicle; however, the noun *ride* usually means an attraction at an amusement park. Below is a list of easily confused verbs:

adapt — adopt	*acquire — require*	*affect — effect*
assign — consign	*compose — comprise*	*lay — lie*
lend — borrow	*precede — proceed*	*protect — protest*
raise — rise	*remove — move*	*persecute — prosecute*

i) **Inflation ------- the buying power of the dollar.**

(A) affects   (B) deletes

(C) effects   (D) completes

Warm-ups

1. We will have to ------- a new marketing strategy to sell that product overseas.

   (A) adept   (B) adopt
   (C) adapt   (D) edict

2. Our legal department will aggressively ------- any copyright violations.

   (A) persecute   (B) process
   (C) prosecute   (D) produce

3. As of next week, all workers will be ------- to wear hard hats while operating the forklifts.

   (A) sequestered   (B) requited
   (C) acquired   (D) required

Nouns

A common problem when choosing the correct noun is the confusion caused by similar prefixes and suffixes. Words that end in *-ment* don't necessarily have the same or similar meanings. The same is true with endings such as *-ate, -ish, -ise/-ize,* etc. It is important to pay attention to the root word, not the attachment. Below is a list of easily confused nouns:

aid — aide	*consul — council*	*moral — morale*
alley — ally	*corporation — cooperation*	*neighbor — neighborhood*
assay — essay	*crown — clown*	*principal — principle*
capital — capitol	*desert — dessert*	*trail — trial*
complement — compliment	*hall — hole*	

i) His only ------- about his job is that he has to work on Saturdays.

(A) complaint   (B) complement

(C) compliment   (D) accomplishment

Warm-ups

1. All ------- are asked to show up by 10:00 a.m.

   (A) personnel   (B) personnels
   (C) personalities   (D) personal

2. I'm afraid we'll have to cancel the new project. We can't raise enough
   -------.

   (A) capital   (B) captain
   (C) capitol   (D) capon

3. Under the new contract, everyone will get a 5% -------.

   (A) praise   (B) rise
   (C) access   (D) raise

Modifiers

Choosing the correct modifier can sometimes be confusing. An important thing to consider is whether the word to be modified is *countable* or *uncountable.* Below is a list of modifiers:

- adjectives to be used with countable nouns:
  — *many, a few, few, the fewest, more, a number of, a lot of*
- adjectives to be used with uncountable nouns:
  — *much, a great deal of, a little, little, less, the least, a lot of, more*
- adjectives to be used with singular countable nouns:
  — *each, every, either, neither, another*

TIPS

• Information is uncountable (i.e., we cannot say, "one information," "several informations," etc.) so *another* and *every* do not qualify as its modifiers. Responses (B) *farther* and (C) *further* are similar in meaning, but *farther* almost always relates to physical distance. Therefore, (C) is correct.

i) **For ------- information, call us at 1-800-354-1114.**

(A) another   (B) farther
(C) further   (D) every

Warm-ups

1. Oh no! I don't have ------- time to prepare for the job interview.

   (A) some   (B) much
   (C) very   (D) many

2. I was ------- busy that I forgot to take my lunch break.

   (A) very   (B) much
   (C) such   (D) so

3. She spoke ------- firmly to him about his poor job performance.

   (A) most   (B) quite
   (C) quiet   (D) little

Conjunctions and Conjunctive Adverbs

Conjunctions are relationship words that logically connect elements in a sentence, while conjunctive adverbs express the relationship between independent sentences. Conjunctions do not always have to come in the middle of a sentence; they can come at the beginning of a sentence to show emphasis. Below is a brief list of conjunctions and conjunctive adverbs:

- Conjunctions: *and, but, for, nor, or, so, yet, as, because, if, provided that, than*

- Conjunctive adverbs: *also, as a result, consequently, either, however, in fact, moreover, neither, nevertheless, therefore, thus*

TIPS

- The clue is the presence of *neither* in the initial position— remember what is compatible with *neither*. Therefore, (C) is correct. Pairs such as the following are also worth your attention: *either ~ or ~, both ~ and ··, ·· and similarly.*

i) Neither the CEO ------- the board of directors is opposed to our plan.

(A) and

(B) or

(C) nor

(D) but

Warm-ups

1. ------- your office switches to QuickPhone PremiumPlus, you will get better long distance rates.

    (A) Yet

    (B) For

    (C) If

    (D) In fact

2. My boss was just selected as the new regional manager. -------, his old position is now open.

    (A) For

    (B) Yet

    (C) Thus

    (D) Or

3. The new advertising slogan will be, "Beppos tastes good ------- a peanut butter should."

    (A) just as

    (B) although

    (C) because

    (D) but

Prepositions

Prepositions, like conjunctions, help establish the relationship between elements of a sentence. Below is a list of prepositions:

in, at, of, by, for, beneath, because of, in spite of, considering, except, than, as, before

TIPS

• Answer (B) *by* is correct because the blank space needs a preposition denoting "means." Answer (A) *at* denotes "location" and answers (C) *toward* and (D) *along* denote "movement."

i) Please have these documents sent out immediately ------- express mail.

(A) at   (B) by
(C) toward   (D) along

Warm-ups

1. ------- the bad weather, I was forced to reschedule the business meeting in Thailand.

   (A) Regarding   (B) From
   (C) Because   (D) Because of

2. Do what you want, but ------- for me, I won't sign until I've read the entire contract.

   (A) as   (B) because
   (C) in the case   (D) about

3. ------- for the long drive every morning, I really like my new job.

   (A) Accept   (B) Except
   (C) Although   (D) Not including

Question Type 2

Grammar Questions

Verbs

Verbs express existence, action, or occurrence. They change their form depending on the subject, which is called number agreement between subject and verb. Additionally, verbs help identify whether an action has happened in the past, is happening now, or will happen in the future; this is called the *tense* of the verb.

i) Theodore will ------- the delivery truck after lunch.

   (A) fixing   (B) fixed

   (C) fix   (D) fixes

ii) I am ------- my supervisor with job interviews.

   (A) help   (B) will help

   (C) helped   (D) helping

- *Fix* is the base form of the verb. When the verb is in this form, it is able to take the future modal *will*. (A) is incorrect because it uses the *-ing* form of the verb. The *-ing* form of the verb cannot be paired with *will*. (B) is incorrect because it is in the past tense when the sentence indicates a future action. (D) is incorrect because the verb is in the third person *-s* form. The *-s* form cannot be paired with *will*.

- The word to focus on in this sentence is *am*. Only response (D) *helping* can follow *am* in this sentence. None of the other forms of *help* are possible with *am*. Here *be + ~ing* makes the present continuous.

Warm-ups

1. Can you please ------- a message for me?

   (A) have taken   (B) take

   (C) taken   (D) took

2. All employees must ------- their cars in Lot B next to the main building.

   (A) parked   (B) to park

   (C) park   (D) have parked

TIPS

• The speaker's vacation is over. Therefore, it is necessary that she return to work tomorrow. Responses (B) and (C) are incorrect because *might* and *could* suggest that the speaker has an option to either return to work or not return to work. Answer (A) is the correct answer because the modal *must* is used to indicate necessity, or something one has to do. (D) is incorrect because it is in the past tense, and the sentence refers to the future.

TIPS

• Answer (C) is the correct answer because the modal *can* indicates choice. (A) is incorrect because *must* indicates necessity. (B) is incorrect because *should* indicates the better or suggested course of action within a group of options. (D) is incorrect because a past tense form is not appropriate here.

Auxiliary Verbs

An important type of auxiliary verb is the modal auxiliary. Modals are words such as *could, will, should, might,* etc, and are used to express such things as permission, ability, and necessity. It is important for the learner to note that sometimes changing the modal can drastically affect the meaning of the sentence!

i) **Today is the last day of my vacation. I ------- go back to work tomorrow.**

(A) must (B) might

(C) could (D) had

ii) **We ------- choose the dental insurance program or the $2,000 bonus, but not both.**

(A) must (B) should

(C) can (D) didn't

Warm-ups

1. ------- I show you some photos of my family?

(A) Must (B) Would

(C) Shall (D) Have

2. The meeting is in one hour. I ------- finish this report now!

(A) must (B) ought

(C) can (D) might

Subject - verb Agreement

Subjects and verbs are said to *agree* when they match in number; i.e., a singular subject needs a singular verb, and a plural subject takes a plural verb. In particular, look for clues like the third person singular -s (e.g., *She goes. He works.*).

i) Every Christmas she ------- money to charity.

(A) give
(B) gives
(C) given
(D) giving

ii) One of the lawyers ------- an accountant, too.

(A) is
(B) are
(C) am
(D) to be

- (B) is the correct answer because the verb *gives* agrees with the subject *she* (I give, She/He/It gives, We give, You give, They give). (A) is incorrect because the verb is not in agreement with the subject. Responses (C) and (D) are incorrect because of tense and lack of auxiliary verbs.

- The correct answer is (A). It is important not to be distracted by the word closest to the verb. In this case, *lawyers* is plural, so the tendency may be to use the verb form *are*. However, the sentence says "*One* of the lawyers..." For this reason, (B) is incorrect. (C) is incorrect because the verb *am* is conjugated for the subject I. (D) *to be* is simply the infinitive form of the verb *be* and not appropriate here.

Warm-ups

1. All the workers in that division ------- moving to a new office.

(A) is
(B) am
(C) are
(D) are going to

2. My boss ------- golf very well.

(A) playing
(B) play
(C) can plays
(D) plays

TIPS

- (A) *advertise* and (B) *to advertise* are incorrect because an infinitive cannot be used to modify a noun that follows it. (D) is incorrect because what is advertised is not the strategy itself but products or goods. Answer (C) is correct because the gerund *advertising* is used to construct a noun phrase: *advertising strategy*. Note that in this case *advertising* also acts as an adjective modifying the word "strategy."

TIPS

- Answer (B) is correct because it includes the infinitive marker *to*, which is needed to establish a relationship between the subject and the action. (A) is incorrect because it lacks the necessary infinitive marker. (C) is incorrect because it repeats the future indicative *will*. (D) is incorrect because it mixes the infinitive marker *to* with the continuous tense *-ing*.

Gerunds and Infinitives

Gerunds, sometimes called a nominal present participle, are verbs used as subjects, objects, complements and in other roles. For example in the sentence, "Swimming is good exercise," *swimming* is a gerund. While in the sentence, "He went swimming after lunch," *swimming* is a continuous form of the verb.

Infinitives are the base form of the verb preceded by the infinitive marker *to*. Infinitives can be confusing because sometimes they omit the infinitive marker in writing or speaking, though it remains implied.

i) **Her ------- strategy was the most successful in the history of her company.**

    (A) advertise   (B) to advertise

    (C) advertising   (D) advertised

ii) **He will be asked ------- a presentation at next month's staff meeting.**

    (A) give   (B) to give

    (C) will give   (D) to giving

Warm-ups

1. ------- is one office skill that I'm not very good at.

    (A) To type   (B) Typing

    (C) Doing typing   (D) Good typist

2. I have to go to the donut factory ------- their inventory.

    (A) checking   (B) to check

    (C) to checking   (D) will check

Nouns and Pronouns

Nouns are people, places, things, and ideas. Sometimes, writers and speakers find it awkward to repeat the same noun over and over again. In these cases, pronouns are used to take the place of nouns.

i) Our company sponsors many of the ------- at the new amusement park.

(A) rode   (B) rides

(C) riding   (D) ride

ii) Mom's Famous Cakes is a very well respected company. ------- was founded in 1906 by Margaret Dennison.

(A) She   (B) They

(C) Mom's Famous Cakes   (D) It

TIPS

- This sentence needs a noun. Answer (B) is correct because *ride* is a word that is used as both a noun and a verb. In the case of this sentence, *rides* are the attractions at an amusement park. Because response (A) is a verb, it can't be preceded by an article *the*. Response (C) *riding* is a continuous verb, not a noun. (D) is incorrect because *ride* is singular and the sentence needs a plural noun.

TIPS

- Answer (D) is the correct answer because *Mom's Famous Cakes* is the name of a singular company. Thus it takes the pronoun *it*. (A) is incorrect because *She* refers to a female person, not a company named after a female person. (B) is incorrect because the company is a singular, not plural, noun. (C) is incorrect because after a proper noun is presented, it is usually replaced with a pronoun in the following sentence to prevent too much repetition of the same words.

Warm-ups

1. Mrs. Smythe is in charge of personnel. ------- does all of the hiring for the company.

   (A) He   (B) I

   (C) She   (D) It

2. The advertising division is concerned about the new product. They think ------- will not sell very well.

   (A) them   (B) that

   (C) they   (D) it

TIPS

- Answer (C) is the correct answer because the conjunction *but* shows contrast. (A) is incorrect because *and* is used to indicate similar or connected conditions. (B) is incorrect because *so* indicates a result or outcome, and the sentence does not specify any outcome from getting a promotion. (D) is incorrect because *or* indicates choice, or options.

TIPS

- Answer (B) is the correct answer because the conjunction *so* indicates a result or outcome. Taking a vacation in February can be seen as the outcome of being busy in January. (A) is incorrect because *or* indicates choice, which the sentence does not specify. Responses (C) and (D) are incorrect because they both indicate contrast, which is not shown in the sentence. Furthermore, *however* is not a conjunction but a conjunctive adverb.

Conjunctions

Conjunctions are words that connect clauses within a single idea. Below is a list of conjunctions:

- Coordinating conjunctions: *and, but, for, nor, or, so, yet*

- Subordinating conjunctions: *as, although, because, if, though, unless, when, while*

i) **We were both hoping to be promoted. I got a promotion, ------- my assistant did not.**

(A) and   (B) so

(C) but   (D) or

ii) **My company is very busy in January, ------- I'll take a vacation in February.**

(A) or   (B) so

(C) but   (D) however

Warm-ups

1. I forgot my credit card, ------- I'll have to pay with cash.

(A) but   (B) and

(C) if   (D) so

2. You should have enough space on that table, ------- if you don't, you can use my desk as well.

(A) but   (B) so

(C) or   (D) furthermore

Comparatives and Superlatives

Comparatives contrast and rank two nouns. Superlatives contrast and rank three or more nouns.

- Comparative forms include
  adj./adv. *-er* than
  adj./adv. *-ier* than
  more/less adj./adv. than
- Superlative forms include
  the adj./adv. *-est*
  the adj./adv. *-iest*
  the most/least adj./adv.

i) My new computer is far ------- than my old one.

(A) best   (B) good
(C) better   (D) greater

ii) She is ------- supervisor I've ever worked for.

(A) best   (B) better
(C) the better   (D) the best

• Responses (A) and (B) are not comparative forms. (D) is incorrect because *greater* is not a good word choice. (C) is the correct answer because the sentence is comparing two things.

• Response (D) is the correct answer because *ever* requires a superlative with the definite article *the*. (A) is incorrect because the superlative is not preceded by *the*. Finally, (B) and (C) are incorrect because the sentence does not involve a comparison between two nouns.

Warm-ups

1. This new office is much ------- than my old office.

   (A) nice   (B) nicest
   (C) the nicest   (D) nicer

2. Don't save ------- work for last. Get started on it early.

   (A) most difficult   (B) the most difficult
   (C) the more difficult   (D) mostly difficult

Answer Key
1. D 2. B

Negation

Negation is the use of the negative, or saying *no*. Negations do not always use a negative word such as *no* or *not*.

> The following adverbs are already negative in sense, so you should not use a negative form with them: *never, rarely, hardly, barely, seldom, scarcely*

TIPS

• (B) is the correct answer because *hardly* has a negative sense. (A) and (C) are not possible because the word *hardly* can't be used with a negative form. (D) is incorrect because *spoke* is the past form.

i) I ------- hardly understand him because he spoke too quickly.

(A) couldn't   (B) could

(C) can't   (D) can

TIPS

• Answer (A) is the correct answer because it matches the tag question *are you?* (B) is incorrect because the tag question *are you?* is a positive form, so a negative form should be used here. (C) is incorrect because it is both a positive form and past tense. (D) is incorrect because the tense is past and does not match the tag.

ii) You ------- coming to the office Christmas party, are you?

(A) aren't   (B) are

(C) were   (D) weren't

Warm-ups

1. I decided that ------- would be the better decision.
   (A) not go   (B) to going
   (C) not going   (D) going not

2. I warned him ------- release the statistics until next week.
   (A) not   (B) don't
   (C) not to   (D) to

Sample Test: PART 5

Choose the word or phrase that best completes the sentence.

1. All attendees are advised not to -------
   the subject of the meeting to anyone
   else.
   (A) discourse
   (B) disclose
   (C) display
   (D) discard

2. Call the repair person. The ------- is
   tearing the papers again.
   (A) coffee
   (B) paper
   (C) copier
   (D) document

3. My wife and I ------- the company picnic
   last weekend.
   (A) were attending
   (B) attend
   (C) attended
   (D) attending

4. The key to the restroom is on a chain
   ------- the wall in the lunchroom.
   (A) over
   (B) on
   (C) at
   (D) in

5. Turn in your expense report by the 18ᵗʰ,
   ------- you won't get any money back.
   (A) if
   (B) although
   (C) or
   (D) nor

6. All of the legal terms in this contract are
   ------- my head.
   (A) on
   (B) under
   (C) over
   (D) in front of

7. Sarah was moved to the office ------- by
   the window.
   (A) companion
   (B) compartment
   (C) cubicle
   (D) cuticle

8. Please ------- all your business expenses
   from your monthly expense report.
   (A) deduct
   (B) deduce
   (C) induct
   (D) induce

9. My desk drawers are full of -------.
   (A) odds and ends
   (B) spic and spans
   (C) do's and don'ts
   (D) ins and outs

10. We may as well ------- some coffee; we'll
    be working on these reports all night.
    (A) blew
    (B) brew
    (C) stew
    (D) do

11. They made me shift manager. I now have eight people ------- me.

   (A) over
   (B) under
   (C) between
   (D) beside

12. You could just forget the situation, ------- I would fill out an accident report just in case.

   (A) therefore
   (B) if
   (C) and
   (D) but

13. Tomorrow, the company will ------- which workers will be laid off.

   (A) announce
   (B) propose
   (C) denounce
   (D) deduce

14. ------- difficult things may be, you are lucky to have that job.

   (A) But
   (B) So
   (C) However
   (D) Though

15. Which do you like -------, the black or the brown leather briefcase?

   (A) good
   (B) the most
   (C) the better
   (D) better

16. Did you really read the office memo, ------- did you just throw it in the trash?

   (A) but
   (B) however
   (C) therefore
   (D) or

17. ------- coming into work today because I am sick.

   (A) I am
   (B) I will
   (C) I'm not
   (D) I didn't

18. The toilets in the upstairs office are much ------- than the ones in this office.

   (A) clean
   (B) cleaner
   (C) cleanliness
   (D) cleaned

19. I was angry, ------- I said to him, "I'm busy. Get someone else to file your papers!"

   (A) nevertheless
   (B) yet
   (C) additionally
   (D) so

20. Our office is easy to find. It's ------- building in the city.

   (A) the taller
   (B) taller
   (C) the tallest
   (D) the tall

21. Your presentation was well planned, ------- a little difficult to understand.

    (A) but
    (B) and
    (C) then
    (D) therefore

22. The legal case I'm working on this month is much ------- interesting than the one I worked on last month.

    (A) the most
    (B) more
    (C) the more
    (D) most

23. No, I ------- think that an office assistant would be useful.

    (A) don't
    (B) does
    (C) doesn't
    (D) am doing

24. That was ------- expensive business trip I've ever been on.

    (A) the most
    (B) the more
    (C) mostly
    (D) most

25. ------- before the promotion board was one of the most stressful things I have ever done.

    (A) Going
    (B) Doing
    (C) Attending
    (D) Having

26. Here at the law firm of Krause, Hopke, Ganly, and Smith, ------- motto is, "The law is for everyone, not just the wealthy."

    (A) their
    (B) our
    (C) its
    (D) my

27. I forgot that this is a non-smoking area. There is no place for me to put my cigarette -------.

    (A) butt
    (B) stick
    (C) remains
    (D) leftovers

28. She was pleased ------- been recommended for the job.

    (A) to have
    (B) to had
    (C) to has
    (D) to having

29. Tell the driver not to park here. It is a loading -------.

    (A) place
    (B) palace
    (C) zone
    (D) tray

30. Go tell ------- to come in now. The meeting is about to start.

    (A) us
    (B) they
    (C) them
    (D) those

31. The corporate policy is against ------- stock in competing companies.

   (A) doing
   (B) holding
   (C) participating in
   (D) being

32. When she told me I got the job, I was so excited that I didn't know what -------.

   (A) to tell
   (B) to talk
   (C) to say
   (D) to speak

33. I was feeling ------- sick, so I went home early.

   (A) little
   (B) a little
   (C) much
   (D) a lot

34. ------- a photographer is one of the most exciting jobs in the world.

   (A) Doing
   (B) Seeing
   (C) Being
   (D) Making

35. Annette was ------- glad to quit her job that she did not even clean out her locker before she left.

   (A) very
   (B) so
   (C) such
   (D) really

36. The company ------- taking the stand that even being five minutes late is the same as missing a day's work.

   (A) is
   (B) will
   (C) am
   (D) isn't

37. I ------- not be able to attend the conference. I have to check my schedule and get back to you.

   (A) must
   (B) could
   (C) can
   (D) might

38. He is our best writer. He ------- the work of three people.

   (A) do
   (B) does
   (C) makes
   (D) make

39. I ------- to apply for the new position. I definitely have the qualifications.

   (A) would
   (B) ought
   (C) may
   (D) should

40. I usually eat my lunch in the breakroom, but today I ------- my lunch at my desk.

   (A) eat
   (B) ate
   (C) eaten
   (D) have eaten

PART 6 Incomplete Texts

Strategies

This section of the TOEIC® checks your ability to choose words and phrases appropriate for a given context. It tests your knowledge and understanding of both vocabulary and grammar. To score well on this section, you should therefore brush up on the common vocabulary themes presented in TOEIC® readings. Below is a simple checklist which should help with the types of questions often included in this section.

Test-taking Tips

- ✓ Look at the choices of words in relation to surrounding words (consider possible collocations).
- ✓ Pay attention to word forms: what kind of word is needed—verb, adjective or noun? Does the context call for a singular or plural noun? Is a count or non-count noun needed?
- ✓ Are there any words among the choices which seem irrelevant in this context? Eliminate such words first.
- ✓ Check any questions given in the text against the types of questions you know.

Vocabulary Themes

Theme 1 — Banking and Finance
Theme 2 — Marketing
Theme 3 — Hospitality
Theme 4 — Office
Theme 5 — Shopping
Theme 6 — Transportation

Theme 7 — Health
Theme 8 — Telephone
Theme 9 — Travel
Theme 10 — Mail
Theme 11 — Insurance
Theme 12 — Meetings

TIPS

1. To "acknowledge receipt of" something is a set expression. Therefore, (B) is the only possible answer.

2. While (A), (B), (C), and (D) can all be followed by the preposition *out*, only (B) makes sense in the context.

Theme 1

Banking and Finance

accounting	debit card	interest rates	standing order
balance	denomination	loans	statement
bureau de change	deposit	mortgage	tax
cash	deposit ceiling	overdraft	transfer
checking account	direct debit	payee	traveler's checks
clerk	exchange rate	remittance	withdraw
currency	interest	savings account	withdrawal

Dear Mrs. Morgan,

This is to 1. ------- receipt of your request to cancel your monthly direct debit

(A) recognize   (B) acknowledge   (C) show   (D) realize

payment to Blake Enterprises. Please come at your earliest convenience to any branch of Smithfords Bank, and one of our clerks will assist you in 2. ------- out

(A) holding   (B) filling   (C) breaking   (D) taking

the necessary forms to authorize cancellation.

Sincerely,

Anthony Milton,
Smithfords Bank

Warm-ups

> **To:** All employees
> **From:** Head Office
> **Re:** Savings Accounts
>
> Please note the new 1. ------- rates and deposit ceilings for the following
>
> (A) exchange   (B) interest   (C) loan   (D) check
>
> savings accounts:
> Saver Plus — balances over $10,000: 2.75% p.a./balances over $25,000: 2.15% p.a. This account no longer has a deposit 2. -------.
>
> (A) roof   (B) ceiling   (C) cover   (D) overdraft
>
> 30 Day Savings — balances over $25,000: 3% p.a./balances over $100,000: 3.15% p.a. This account retains its current deposit ceiling of $500,000.
> 90 Day Savings — (previously known as "90 Day Gold") balances over $100,000: 3.5% p.a./ balances over $250,000: 3.75% p.a. The new deposit ceiling is $750,000.
> Changes are 3. ------- from the first of next month.
>
> (A) collective   (B) affective   (C) effective   (D) terminated

Theme 2
Marketing

advertising	*demand*	*product*	*sales force*
advertisement	*distribution*	*profit*	*strategy*
brand	*innovation*	*promotion*	*supplier*
competition	*management*	*purchase*	*supply*
competitor	*marketer*	*resources*	*target market*
customer satisfaction	*objectives*	*revenue*	

Memo

To: All Customer Service Staff
From: Zadie Boyle
Re: Customer Satisfaction

We will be having a meeting at 9:30 on June 5th to discuss revising our current targets for customer satisfaction. Sales have been falling in recent months, and customer comments 1. ------- us to believe that our customers feel we do not

(A) show   (B) lead   (C) hold   (D) suggest

2. ------- as good a service as the competition. We will have a brainstorming session

(A) make   (B) produce   (C) create   (D) provide

at the meeting, so bring along some good ideas.

TIPS

1. We *lead* someone to believe (something). Therefore, (B) is correct.

2. The verb usually collocated with a *service* is *provide*. Therefore, (D) is correct.

Warm-ups

The deadline for 1. ------- for the in-house "Innovation in Marketing" contest

(A) submissions   (B) attempts   (C) participants   (D) marketers

has been postponed to March 22nd. We are looking for original ideas for our new online advertising campaign. The advertising department is accepting ideas from all Medco employees in an 2. ------- to reflect the true face of our

(A) effect   (B) attempt   (C) acceptance   (D) afford

company and the people who work for it. We want to convey to the public that we are a caring company, not just 3. ------- on profits. We also want to

(A) decided   (B) efforts   (C) focused   (D) concentrated

show that we are the best at what we do.

Entries should be sent via email to the advertising department at medcoiinm@medco.com.

TIPS

1. Responses (B), (C), and (D) are all words that follow *take;* however, only *advantage* makes sense here. Therefore, (C) is the correct answer.

2. We usually *claim* something we are entitled to, such as a free gift or prize. Therefore, (B) is the correct answer.

Theme 3

Hospitality

bartender	customer service	landlord	reservation
beverages	entertainment	(hotel) lobby	seasonal work
catering	food hygiene	porter	serve
cocktail lounge	front desk	premises	snacks
complimentary	head chef	reception	take an order
conference	housekeeper	receptionist	welcoming

Notice

The management of Fordworth Industries would like to invite all workers and their family members to take 1. ------- of the complimentary movie tickets now available

(A) use   (B) hold   (C) advantage   (D) photos

every Wednesday afternoon at the reception desk in the lobby of the employee leisure center. To thank you for all your hard work, we are offering free movie tickets every Wednesday from now until the end of the year. To 2. ------- your tickets, simply

(A) take   (B) claim   (C) pick   (D) realize

show your leisure center membership card to the receptionists, and they will be happy to give you your tickets. We regret that we can only allow a maximum of 4 tickets per family. Enjoy your free movies!

Warm-ups

Please note that the serving of alcoholic beverages to minors will not be 1. -------.

(A) exclaimed   (B) tolerated   (C) treated   (D) checked

The owner of any licensed 2. ------- caught allowing the sale of alcohol to anyone

(A) premises   (B) location   (C) driver   (D) reception

under the age of 21 will be fined a minimum of $500. In order to prevent the accidental sale of alcohol to minors, it is essential that all bartenders and servers check the ID of customers who appear to be in their twenties or younger. While this may be time-consuming, please explain to customers that it is necessary. Customers who refuse to comply should not be allowed to order alcoholic beverages. We understand that you may feel uncomfortable enforcing this system, but it is a legal requirement. Thank you for your 3. -------.

(A) cooperate   (B) cooperated   (C) cooperation   (D) cooperating

Theme 4

Office

account	director	personnel officer	seminar
accountant	document	photocopier	stationery
administration	executive	profession	supervisor
agenda	flex-time	promotion	take maternity leave
conference	intern	résumé	take sick leave
department	job applications	secretary	work nine to five

Memo

To: All staff
From: Personnel
Re: Interns
Date: May 30th

This is just to remind everyone that the internship season is with us again. We will be welcoming 10 interns from the local high school during their summer vacation. There will be one intern in each department, for four weeks. 1. ------- are copies of

(A) Connected   (B) Attached   (C) Stuck   (D) Joined

their résumés, for your reference. Please be friendly to them and let them know what it is really like to work for a publishing company. Our interns were 2. ------- from the

(A) picking   (B) selected   (C) preferred   (D) elected

top students at St. Hadrian's, and they are very enthusiastic about coming here.

TIPS

1. The word *attached* is commonly used when an additional paper or document accompanies another.

2. Although all the words are connected to the idea of choice, (B) is the most appropriate word choice.

Warm-ups

This month's meeting will be held on Wednesday March 13th at 4:00 p.m. in the small meeting room. The following items are to be 1. -------. This is to be a

(A) talked   (B) spoken about   (C) discussed   (D) gossiped about

fairly informal meeting, and it is hoped it will be over by 5:30.
New Business

- Changes to maternity and paternity leave regulations--extension of period
- New positions – 2. ------- for applications

(A) limit   (B) time up   (C) end   (D) deadline

- "Women in Advertising" conference presentations
- Feedback on 3. ------- introduction of flex-time for all full-time workers

(A) suggestion   (B) indicated   (C) implied   (D) proposed

Committee reports (no reports to be given this month)
Any other business - feel free to bring up anything you feel needs discussing

TIPS

1. *Draw (someone's) attention to something* is a commonly used set expression. Therefore, (C) is the correct answer.

2. *Until further notice* is another set expression. Therefore, (C) is the correct answer.

Theme 5

Shopping

aisle	counter	loyalty card	shopping mall
barcode	customer relations	opening hours	stock
bargain	customer service	refund	store credit
cash register	damaged	reputation	try on
changing room	discount	shelves	undersold
clerk	display		

Notice

Monkfields Grocers would like to **1.** ------- customers' attention to the information

(A) pull   (B) assist   (C) draw   (D) make

below.

Due to current staff shortages owing to sickness, we would like you to note the following changes to our hours: From Monday January 30ᵗʰ until further **2.** -------, we will be opening at 9:00 a.m., instead of 8:00 a.m., and will be closing at 7:00 p.m.,

(A) attention   (B) sign   (C) notice   (D) opinion

instead of 8:30. We apologize for any inconvenience, and will return to our regular hours as soon as possible.

Warm-ups

To: GraceBros@gracebros.com
From: misco@hotnet.com
Date: Sept. 23
Subject: Complaint

Dear Sirs,
As a(n) **1.** ------- customer at Grace Brothers Department Store, I feel compelled

(A) regular   (B) ordinary   (C) normal   (D) often

to complain about the recent increase in prices. I have always considered your store to be of a high quality, but with reasonable prices. However, over the past few months, I have noticed that your prices have been creeping up. This week I went to purchase a cosmetic product which I buy, on **2.** -------,

(A) median   (B) medium   (C) average   (D) usually

about 4 times a year. Of course I like prices to remain static, but this time the price had risen by over 50%. I saw the same item on sale at a much lower price in a **3.** ------- store. Needless to say, I bought the cheaper item.

(A) contender   (B) competitor   (C) peer   (D) rival

I am not sure what explanation you can offer, but I just wanted to let you know how I feel.

Sincerely,

Cynthia Carter

Answer Key
1 A 2 C 3 D

Theme 6

Transportation

access	ferry	passenger	subway
arrival	freight	rail pass	to fly
cancellation	highway	runway	to land
congestion	interchange	schedule	to take off
delay	intersection	seat reservation	transit
departure	long-distance bus	station	

Dear Maria,

This is just to let you know that the representatives from the head office will be 1. -------

(A) landing   (B) driving   (C) flying   (D) leaving

into Heathrow Airport. They are scheduled to land at Terminal 2 at 3:00 p.m. on Monday. I have sent them details on how to get to the office by subway, so they can make their own way here. They will call you when they get on the subway, so could you please 2. ------- them at the station and bring them here?

(A) pick   (B) gather   (C) take   (D) meet

Many thanks,

Victor

TIPS

1. We *fly into* but *land at* an airport, we *leave from* somewhere, and we might *drive to* an airport; therefore, response (C) is the correct choice.

2. Responses (A) and (B) do not make sense here. Response (C) could be the right answer, if the blank were followed by a phrase "from the station," not by "at the station." Therefore, response (D), *meet*, is the only option.

Warm-ups

Would passengers please note that from October 22ⁿᵈ, all seats on the Star Liner Express will require reservations between 7:30 and 9:00 a.m., and again from 5:00 to 7:00 p.m. This is due to the great 1. ------- for seats at

(A) demand   (B) command   (C) claim   (D) wish

these times of day, and new safety regulations which restrict the number of standing passengers allowed to board the train. Reservations may be made by telephone in 2. -------, or in person on the day of travel. Monthly rail pass holders

(A) prior   (B) advance   (C) before   (D) ahead

are also required to make reservations for journeys made during these times. There will be no additional 3. ------- for reservations.

(A) cost   (B) fine   (C) price   (D) charge

We would like to apologize for any inconvenience and thank you for using South Coast Railways.

Answer Key: 1 A 2 B 3 D

89

TIPS

1. The correct answer is (D). (C) is wrong because there is no such concept as *cardiovasculars*. Answer (A) is another word for health club, and answer (B) helps build strength, not cardiovascular fitness.

2. The correct answer is (B). Answers (A), (C), and (D) do not help build muscular strength.

Theme 7

Health

ache	diabetes	nutritional supplements
bench press	diet	personal trainer
blood pressure cuff	eye chart	Pilates
caffeine	free weights	positive visualization
calories	gym/health club	protein
carbohydrates	high/low blood pressure	running machine
cardiovascular	low/high blood sugar	sore
check-up	muscles	stethoscope
cross training	nutrition	yoga

Notice to all employees

As part of McTaggart Corporation's new employee fitness program, a new company health club will be available on the third floor for all employees to use. The health club will include six **1.** ------- to help increase cardiovascular fitness, as well as

(A) a gym   (B) free weights   (C) cardiovasculars   (D) running machines

2. ------- to help develop muscular strength. We hope all employees will take advantage

(A) caffeine   (B) free weights   (C) a running machine   (D) a stethoscope

of this great opportunity to get healthier.

Warm-ups

> ### Notice to all employees
>
> Friday, December 6, a health screening van will be parked in the front parking lot from approximately 9:00 a.m. to 3:00 p.m. The health screening van will be staffed by three nurses as well as a physician's assistant. They will be checking **1.** ------- and blood sugar levels, as well as giving
>
> (A) stethoscope   (B) blood pressure   (C) nurses   (D) blood pressure cuff
>
> information on **2.** -------. There will also be a personal trainer from Roger Platz's
>
> (A) eye chart   (B) free weights   (C) nutrition   (D) running machines
>
> Health and Fitness to talk about the importance of **3.** ------- on a healty lifestyle.
>
> (A) exercise   (B) free weights   (C) muscles   (D) carbohydrates
>
> To allow as many people as possible to attend this health screening, all shift supervisors will be directed to give their workers an additional 30 minutes of break time.

Theme 8

Telephone

analog	dial tone	operator	speed dial
answering machine	digital	phone cord	telephone booth
busy signal	domestic	receiver	trace (a call)
call back service	earpiece	redial	voice message
calling card	hang up	redirect a call	wrong number
cassette	international	rolodex	
crank call	memo	rotary phone	

Memo

To: Stacy Darby, Director, Planning Division

Ms. Darby,

I tried several times to get in contact with the branch office, but I was unable to make contact. The first number was a 1. -------. It turned out to be the phone number

(A) phone number   (B) dial tone   (C) wrong number   (D) right number

to an auto parts store. The second number was probably the right number, but all I got was a 2. -------. I will try again tomorrow.

(A) busy signal   (B) crank call   (C) telephone line   (D) phone call

J. Fred Peck: Assistant to the Director, Planning Division.

TIPS

1. (C) *wrong number* is the right answer because the phone call was to the branch office, not to an auto parts store.

2. (A) is correct. The writer suggests that the number is correct, but he was unable to complete the phone call.

Warm-ups

Advertisement

As a special limited offer to all Bayside Mutual Insurance Employees, JAM Mobile Phone and Internet Provider is offering half off on 1. ------- and domestic

(A) local   (B) international   (C) national   (D) nationwide

phone calls through the summer. Talk to anyone in the world for half the price! JAM also offers a free 2. ------- service to our Premium Plus Customers

(A) phone   (B) talk   (C) voice message   (D) radio

so that you'll never miss a call. Simply record a message, enter *34 and you can save up to 50 messages. If you sign up before the end of the month, JAM will include a 3. ------- worth 100 minutes of talk time that you can use

(A) telephone   (B) credit card   (C) telephone booth   (D) calling card

from your cell phone, a pay phone, or any phone you wish. So what are you waiting for? Start saving today, with JAM!

TIPS

1. The correct answer is (B). Answers (A) and (C) do not relate directly to airline tickets, while answer (D) doesn't make sense within the context of the passage.

2. The correct answer is (C). Since employees would be the ones having an expense account, answer (C) makes sense within the context of the sentence.

Theme 9

Travel

board (a ship)	credit voucher	information kiosk	red-eye (flight)
book (a ticket)	economy	layover	reservation
cancellation fee	expense account	lobby	shut-eye
car pool	fare zone	overhead compartment	suitcase/trunk
carriage/berth	first class	package tour	surcharge
commuter train	hail (a taxi)	peak season	window/aisle seat
concierge	hostel	purser	

Memo to all regional managers

Just a reminder that 1. ------- airline tickets are not deductible on company expenses.

(A) aisle seat   (B) first class   (C) window seat   (D) economy

The company will only pay the amount of an economy ticket. If employees wish to upgrade, they must pay the additional costs themselves. Regional managers must review their employees' 2. ------- to make sure that this policy is being enforced.

(A) fare zones   (B) credit vouchers   (C) expense accounts   (D) surcharges

Warm-ups

> **To:** Mrs. Peggy Tarant
> **From:** Sunvilla Travel
> **Re:** Confirmation of airline tickets
>
> Mrs. Tarrant,
> This is just to confirm the following: First class reservation on Vision Airlines from Helsinki to Madagascar on the first of April at 8:00 a.m.
> The ticket cost includes a 1. ------- of 100 Kronigs,
>
> (A) reservation   (B) price   (C) cancellation fee   (D) car pool
>
> which is non-refundable. 2. ------- will begin at 7:30 at gate 37 and an
>
> (A) Boarding   (B) Entering   (C) Flying   (D) The day
>
> appointed Sunvilla Travel 3. ------- will be waiting for you upon your arrival at
>
> (A) airplane   (B) package tour   (C) driver   (D) car pool
>
> Madagascar International Airport. Because you are not taking part in a package tour, we suggest you book any travel arrangements that you may plan while in Madagascar through your hotel which, we feel, offers very fair rates and exceptional service.
>
> Thank you for choosing Sunvilla Travel, and we wish you a safe journey.

Answer Key 1 C 2 A 3 C

Theme 10
Mail

airmail	parcel	registered mail
cash on delivery (COD)	post office	return to sender
dead letter office	postal insurance	scale
envelope	postage meter	snail mail
first class	Post Office (PO) Box	(to) sort
fragile	postcard	stamp
metered mail	postmark	weigh
mailing restrictions	postmaster	zip code
money order	private courier	zone fare

Inter-office memo

Beginning August 31st, Westmore Home Architecture will no longer use 1. -------.

(A) stamps   (B) stumps   (C) stomps   (D) mail

Instead, when sending letters or packages, we will be using a 2. ------- that will

(A) stamp   (B) marker   (C) postage meter   (D) postage maker

automatically weigh the item being sent, calculate the correct postage, and mark the item accordingly. Training on the new device will begin on Monday.

TIPS

1. The correct answer is (A). Answers (B) and (C) have no connection with sending mail, and answer (D) doesn't make sense within the context of the sentence.

2. The correct answer is (C). Answers (B) and (D) are distracter answers, while (A) does not fit the context of the passage.

Warm-ups

Fax

Mrs. Jameson,

Here is the mailing address for Rossi and Associates in Finland. Please send the completed building plans by 1. ------- with an

(A) private courier   (B) public courier   (C) post office   (D) parcel

2. ------- date of no later than December 14th.

(A) acceptance   (B) attendance   (C) arrival   (D) entry

When we receive the building plans, we will send a 3. ------- for the balance

(A) postal insurance (B) postage meter   (C) money order   (D) postmaster

of the payment. Please do not use the regular postal system, as we feel that it will take too long to arrive, and we will miss our deadline. If you have any questions, please call or fax our branch office in London. They will be able to provide you with further details regarding this project and its deadlines.

Thank you for your assistance,

Roman Transko, Director, Planning Division

TIPS

1. The correct answer is (A). Answers (B) and (D) are both incorrect terms and answer (C) does not fit the context of the passage.

2. The correct answer is (C). Answer (A) would not be a term applied to an insurance premium. Answers (B) and (D) have to do with giving money, whereas the context implies receiving money.

Theme 11

Insurance

borrow	deed	lend	survivor's benefit
cash out	dependents	lien	term
compensation	full coverage	mortgage	terminate
contract	homeowner	partial coverage	underwriter
co-payment	indemnity	policy	widow
cosigner	lapse	premium	widower
deductible	lease	renter	

Notice

All employees hired after September 21ˢᵗ will be covered under the Westbrook Plus life insurance **1.** ------- instead of Westbrook Premium. Westbrook Plus has

(A) policy   (B) deed   (C) police   (D) lease

two advantages. First, it has lower monthly payments, and second, you can **2.** -------

(A) borrow   (B) lease   (C) cash out   (D) buy

your premium any time after the first year. Please see your payroll manager for more details on either Westbrook Plus or Premium.

Warm-ups

Advertisement

Aveno Health, the first name in health insurance, is now offering **1.** -------

(A) health   (B) deductible   (C) cash out   (D) homeowner's

insurance as well. Whether you own your home or **2.** -------, Aveno has a

(A) buy   (B) rent   (C) lend   (D) borrow

policy that is right for you. You can choose either full or partial coverage and you can even set the amount of the **3.** ------- based on how much you can

(A) deductible   (B) money   (C) cash out   (D) fare

pay. Another added benefit is that you can combine your Aveno health insurance payment with your Aveno homeowner's insurance payment and just make one payment per month. Don't miss out on this fantastic opportunity. Remember, Aveno for life—and now property!

Theme 12

Meetings

annually	gavel	pro/con
attend	guest speaker	profit/loss
bi-monthly	itinerary	quarterly
budget	marketing	Research and Development (R & D)
closed-door	merger	seniority
conference	negotiations	sequester
constructive criticism	open-door	team leader
consult	podium/dais	teleconference
evaluation report	presentation	yearly/monthly planner

Notice to set-up crew

The Computer Supplier Conference will be held in the Cherry Jubilee Room. Please arrange the 1. ------- next to the computer terminal because they will be hosting a

(A) dais   (B) chairs   (C) room   (D) conference

2. ------- with suppliers from overseas. The room will need 350 chairs on the floor

(A) meeting   (B) teleconference (C) conference   (D) consultation

and ten chairs up on the stage. Please leave two aisles going from the stage to the rear of the room. If you have questions, contact Mr. Davey.

TIPS

1. The correct answer is (A). The context suggests a single piece of furniture; therefore, (B) is incorrect. Answers (C) and (D) are not tangible objects that could be placed next to the computer terminal.

2. The correct answer is (B). While answers (A), (C), and (D) are possible, they would not need connection to a computer terminal as requested in the notice.

Warm-ups

Notice to all shift managers

As you are probably aware, Sandez Petroleum will be hosting its 1. -------

(A) weeks   (B) annual   (C) month-long   (D) daily

Performance Improvement Meeting and Seminar next month at the Gasparin Hotel on Seaview Road. Please let your workers know that the day has been changed from December 10th to December 17th. This year's meeting and seminar will include an afternoon of 2. ------- such as "Effective Team

(A) meetings   (B) work   (C) itinerary   (D) presentations

Organization," "Giving Constructive Criticism," and "Happy Team, Productive Team." There will also be a special 3. -------, Tom Channing, who will speak

(A) talker   (B) guest speaker   (C) person   (D) event

about overcoming stress in the workplace. We hope you will all be able to attend. Remember to inform your staff about the change in dates.
See you there!

Sample Test: PART 6

Questions 1 through 4 refer to the following notice.

Attention all employees!

In light of recent world events, we would like to ask all of you to be extra vigilant on the shop floor. Please keep an eye open for any ------- bags or packages left anywhere in the

1. (A) unattended
   (B) unwatched
   (C) vacant
   (D) opened

store. This is particularly important as the holiday season approaches, and the store will be getting more crowded. Our customers expect a safe shopping environment, and it is our duty to provide one. It is also important to be ------- of any suspicious behavior.

2. (A) considerate
   (B) aware
   (C) alert
   (D) noticed

Should you notice anyone who is acting oddly, please notify one of the ------- staff. We ask

3. (A) safety
   (B) detective
   (C) security
   (D) consumer

you not to approach any suspicious looking individuals. We also ask that you do not approach any unattended baggage, no matter how innocuous it may appear. It is our wish to prevent any ------- from coming to anyone working or shopping in

4. (A) harm
   (B) damage
   (C) breakage
   (D) wrong

the Fridrew Department store.

Questions 5 through 8 refer to the following letter.

22 High Street
Portley
March 22, 2006

Alex Whitfield,
101 Greenstead
Portley

Dear Mr. Whitfield,

Thank you for your letter of March 17th. We were most disturbed to hear of your -------

5. (A) experiences
   (B) experience
   (C) experiencing
   (D) experienced

while visiting Kim and Sons. It was shocking to learn that one of our clerks had been so rude to you. It is the first time that we have had such a(n) -------. I would like to apologize to you

6. (A) objection
   (B) happening
   (C) effort
   (D) complaint

on behalf of all the members of the Kim business family. We pride ourselves on -------

7. (A) making
   (B) providing
   (C) energizing
   (D) forming

friendly, efficient service with a sincere regard for our customers. I have spoken to the clerk involved, and he admits that what you say is true. He is no longer an -------- here, and

8. (A) employment
   (B) employee
   (C) employer
   (D) employed

I hope that you will not hesitate to return to our store.

Sincerely,

Harold Kim

Questions 9 through 12 refer to the following email.

Date: September 23, 2005
From: Hymills@Mills.com
To: zenap23@happy.co
Subject: Stationary Order

This is just to ------- the order placed over the telephone earlier today. As we discussed

    9. (A) refer
       (B) confirm
       (C) notify
       (D) respect

before, I would like to order the ------- items:

    10. (A) following
        (B) below
        (C) preceding
        (D) under

32 boxes of A4 paper, white, recycled
20 boxes of A4 paper, white (NOT recycled)
2 packs of A4 paper, green
2 boxes of black ball point pens (the cheapest you have in stock)
1 box of red ball point pens
15 large glue sticks, any brand

I would also like to confirm that this order will be ------- to our account, as is our usual

    11. (A) asked
        (B) taken
        (C) charged
        (D) bought

policy. Please send the ------- as soon as it is ready. I need to submit it to the accounting

    12. (A) invoice
        (B) papers
        (C) notice
        (D) arrangement

department before the end of the week.

Thank you for your consideration,
Hayley Mills

1	B	2	A
3	C	4	A
5	B	6	D
7	B	8	B
9	B	10	A
11	C	12	A

Answer Key

98

Reading Comprehension

This section of the TOEIC® assesses your ability to read and understand written English. You must read passages and then answer questions based on what is stated or implied in the passage. The passages will be about a variety of topics and in a variety of formats, including memos, letters, charts, graphs, indexes, tables, and other common methods of presenting information in print.

Test-taking Tips

✓ Quickly read the passage to gain the main idea and general information. At this stage, you may be able to answer some of the questions.

✓ For the remaining questions, read the relevant parts again and look for more specific details which will help you answer the questions.

✓ Do not be misled by the words or phrases from a passage that are repeated in the choices. These may not always be relevant to the answer.

Question Types

Type 1 — Main Idea Questions
Type 2 — Fact and Detail Questions
Type 3 — Inference Questions
Type 4 — Cause and Effect questions

Question Type 1

Main Idea Questions

Main idea questions will ask you about the primary focus of the reading passage. The main idea may be stated overtly—often near the beginning or end of the passage—or it may be implied, so that you must make an inference by depending on the key words or phrases. Typical main idea questions look like the following:

- **What is the purpose of the letter?**
- **What is the message about?**
- **What is the main idea of the passage?**
- **Why did the writer send this fax?**

KEY EXPRESSIONS

- **confirm** — support or establish the certainty of
- **afterwards** — following a particular event, date, or time
- **prove** — turn out to be

Key Information

1, 5
Martina works for a publishing company.

2
A performance is scheduled for the coming Thursday, at 7:30.

3
Dinner is scheduled at La Mirage after the performance.

4
Alice is going to leave on Friday.

<u>**Questions 1 and 2**</u> refer to the following letter.

Dear Alice,

I trust that your meetings have been going well this week. This is just a short note to confirm the plans for Thursday evening. As I mentioned when we met to discuss [1]the color scheme for your book, I have reserved two tickets for this Thursday's *Swan Lake* at the Sydney Arts Center.

The performance begins [2]at 7:30. As I suggested before, let's meet at the theater between 6:30 and 7:00. I will be sending the company's driver to meet you at your hotel at six o'clock. Afterwards, I hope you will be able to join me and our chief editor, Hank Rearden, [3]for supper at La Mirage. Don't hesitate to contact me if there are any problems. This should be a nice relaxing evening before your departure on [4]Friday morning.

Yours truly,

Martina Hayes
[5]Sales Director

1. What is the purpose of the note?
   (A) To extend an invitation   (B) To reply to an invitation
   (C) To confirm plans   (D) To cancel plans

2. Why did Martina Hayes write this letter?
   (A) To notify Alice of a change of plans
   (B) To ensure Alice knows when and where to meet
   (C) To confirm Alice's flight time
   (D) To check that Alice knows where the theater is

Question Type 2
Fact and Detail Questions

PART 7

Reading Comprehension

Type 1   Main Idea Questions
Type 2   Fact and Detail Questions
Type 3   Inference Questions
Type 4   Cause and Effect Questions

Detail questions will ask you about specific details regarding the information given in the reading passage. The formats of detail questions will vary as follows:

- **Who is Collin Baker?**
- **When will they meet?**
- **How long did they wait for the bus?**
- **Where can they get a permit?**
- **What product is going to be made abroad?**
- **How many times has Mr. Green tried to call John?**
- **Which of the following is NOT mentioned/stated?**
- **What time is the flight leaving?**

<u>**Questions 3 and 4**</u> **refer to the following article.**

Without a doubt, the most important part of any job application is the résumé. Along with a cover letter, it is the first impression a prospective employee makes on a potential employer. Therefore, it is important that a résumé provide as much relevant information as possible while remaining [1]brief. A résumé should be no more than one full side of a sheet of paper. All too many candidates make the mistake of submitting several pages which, more often than not, don't even get a second glance.

A résumé must be neatly printed, with [2]at least three-quarter inch margins on all four sides. Use underlining, capital letters and asterisks [3]to highlight important information. A résumé should be single-spaced with an extra line between blocks of information.

Begin a résumé with your name, address, and contact information (e.g., telephone or fax numbers, email address). Do not include age, marital status, or other personal facts. Next, many résumés state the position sought [4]or career goal. Then comes perhaps the most important part: a chronological outline of work experience—starting with the most recent job and working [5]backwards—including for each position a brief description of relevant duties and skills used or acquired. Finally, include an outline of your educational background from the most recent backwards. Make sure to list dates of completion, full names and locations (if not common knowledge) of schools, and diplomas or certificates awarded.

3. Which of the following should NOT be on your résumé?

   (A) Your name and telephone and fax numbers
   (B) The year you received your bachelor's degree
   (C) Your nationality and the fact that you are single
   (D) A description of tasks performed in your last job

4. What is true about a résumé?

   (A) Résumés should be brief but very informative.
   (B) A résumé should have three-quarter inch margins on both sides.
   (C) Important information should be italicized.
   (D) An outline of educational background should end with the most recent information.

KEY EXPRESSIONS

- **prospective** — likely to become or be
- **chronological** — arranged in the order of time of occurrence
- **diploma** — a document issued by a school indicating that the recipient has successfully completed a course of study

Key Information

[1]
A résumé should be brief.

[2]
The margins should be superscript of an inch or more on all four sides.

[3]
Important information should somehow be highlighted.

[4]
A career goal precedes a chronological outline of work experience.

[5]
Outlining of work history and education background should be in reverse chronological order.

PART 7

Reading Comprehension

Type 1 Main Idea Questions
Type 2 Fact and Detail Questions
Type 3 Inference Questions
Type 4 Cause and Effect Questions

Question Type 3

Inference Questions

Inference questions check your ability to use details to draw a logical conclusion based on specific information in the reading. Although the answer is not stated explicitly in the reading passage, the passage will provide you with enough information to choose the correct answer. As in main idea questions and the fact and detail questions, you should look for key words or phrases that will help you to draw a correct conclusion. Typical inference questions may look like the following:

- **Where did the woman used to live?**
- **How often does the man probably play tennis?**
- **It can be inferred from the passage that...**

Questions 5 and 6 refer to the following advertisement and email.

SAVE THIS HOLIDAY SEASON!

For [1]a limited time, the Regal Inn is offering its deluxe family suite [2]for just $159.99—barely half our standard rate! Each unit is nicely appointed with two double beds and a separate living area that includes kitchen facilities and a dining table. When you'd rather have someone else do the cooking for you, enjoy luxurious dining in one of our three award-winning restaurants, or have [3]room service bring you a meal. And between meals, you can work up an appetite [4]in one of our two heated indoor pools or fully-equipped workout room. To make a reservation, call 1-800-555-ROOM or email deluxe.room@regal.co

- Standard rooms available from $99.99.
- Offer good through January 5th

To: deluxe.room@regal.co
From: harrytan@netscap.com
Subject: Reservation

I'd like to make a reservation for a deluxe family suite at the special holiday rate of $159.99. Please make my [5]reservation for December 22nd to December 26th. Please let me know as soon as possible if these dates are available, and I will send you my credit card details.

Thanking you,
Harry Tan

5. Based on the information in the passage, to which holiday does the advertisement refer?

(A) Summer   (B) Christmas
(C) Ramadan   (D) Easter

6. Which of the following can be inferred from the passage about the Regal Hotel?

(A) It is going to increase the family rate.
(B) It is going to provide the guests with a free meal.
(C) It is going to allow the guests to cook in their room.
(D) It is going to close down the outdoor pools temporarily.

KEY EXPRESSIONS

- **deluxe** — particularly elegant and luxurious
- **facility** — something created for a particular function
- **suite** — a hotel unit that includes more than one type of room
- **workout room** — a room with exercise facilities

Key Information

[1]
The hotel adopts a new family rate for the holiday season.

[2]
The rate for a deluxe family suite is $159.99, which is almost half the standard rate.

[3]
The guests can have food delivered to their own rooms.

[4]
Guests can swim and do physical exercise indoors.

[5]
The man wants to reserve a room in December from the 22nd until the 26th.

Question Type 4
Cause and Effect Questions

PART 7

Reading Comprehension

Type 1   Main Idea Questions

Type 2   Fact and Detail Questions

Type 3   Inference Questions

Type 4   Cause and Effect questions

Cause and effect questions look at the reason for an event or action and its consequences. For this type of question, you may find it helpful to look for expressions such as *because (of), due to, owing to, as a result of,* and *thanks to* to focus on cause. Cause and effect questions often take the following forms:

- **Why is traffic heavy on the highway?**
- **What may happen because of the hurricane?**
- **What caused the shipment to arrive late?**

Questions 7 and 8 refer to the following information and letter.

Using City Buses

City Buses are white and blue. Please board at the front door and [1]pay the fare as you get on. The fare per ride is [2]$1.50 for adults, and $1.00 for senior citizens and youths aged 10-16. Children under 10 ride free. The fare may be paid with [3]coins, token, or a bus card. Please pay the exact amount directly into the slot at the top of the fare box. Remember that bills are not accepted, and drivers cannot make change for riders. Pre-paid bus cards may be bought at the main bus terminal, or at any news kiosk. Fares paid using a bus card are 20 cents cheaper than when using cash. When you wish to get off the bus, please [4]notify the driver in advance by pressing one of the buttons located throughout the bus.

Dear City Buses Company,

I am writing to thank you for introducing the city bus pre-paid card. As a senior citizen suffering from arthritis, I have long found it difficult to deal with small coins. In the past, I often dropped my change as I tried to put it into the payment slot, causing a long line of irritated people behind me. This made me reluctant to take the bus, due to my embarrassment. However, [5]the bus card is easy to hold, and it is a wonderful innovation. Many of my older friends have had the same experience, and we are taking the bus more and more often these days.

Thank you,

Hilda Braid

7. What caused Hilda to feel embarrassed when she took the bus?

(A) She didn't have enough coins.

(B) She kept dropping her coins.

(C) She got off at the wrong stop.

(D) She lost her bus card.

8. What has been the result of the introduction of bus cards?

(A) Older people are using the bus more frequently.

(B) Older people no longer use buses.

(C) Hilda Braid has dropped her card.

(D) People have complained because the card is too expensive.

Sample Test: PART 7

Questions 1 through 3 refer to the following fax.

Fax

To: Peter Cooke, Headly Electronics
From: Darren Simpson, Customs and Excise Bureau
Re: Shipment
Date: April 2nd

A shipment of 48 refrigerators has now been cleared for collection by the Dover Port Authority Customs and Excise Bureau. This shipment arrived on March 27th. An import tariff of £13 is payable on each item in the shipment. At £13 x 48 that comes to a total of £634. This is payable before the shipment will be released for collection. Payment should be made to Westman Bank, account #223003, account holder: Custom and Excise. Please fax us once payment has been made.

---

1. What is the purpose of this fax?
   (A) To inform Peter Cooke that his shipment is ready for collection
   (B) To inform Peter Cooke that his shipment has been rejected
   (C) To inform Darren Simpson that he should pay a fee
   (D) To inform Darren Simpson of the cost of a refrigerator

2. Who is Darren Simpson?
   (A) An official at the Customs and Excise Bureau
   (B) An importer of electrical appliances
   (C) A trader
   (D) A banker

3. What should Peter Cooke send after paying the import tariff?
   (A) A letter
   (B) £634
   (C) A fax
   (D) An email

Questions 4 through 6 refer to the following announcement.

Personnel Department News—It gives us great pleasure to announce the appointment of our new vice presidents. As of tomorrow, Marshall and Young, Inc. will have two new vice presidents: Research and Development's Gary Shepherd and Constance Hayes from the Product Design Department, who were informed of their promotions last Tuesday. Mr. Shepherd, who has been with this firm for ten years, will remain in R&D and will be working with Jordan Jones, Senior VP in that department. Ms. Hayes, who has been a Project Manager in Product Design since joining Marshall and Young five years ago, will be heading up the Consumer Products Department along with Eugene Park, who is transferring from his position as vice president in R&D. We are expecting an exciting year and looking forward to the continued success of Mr. Shepherd and Ms. Hayes.

4. How many people from Product Design were promoted?

(A) One
(B) Two
(C) Three
(D) Four

6. When were the new vice-presidents told about the promotion?

(A) Last Tuesday
(B) The day after the vote
(C) Tomorrow
(D) Over a month ago

5. Who will be leading the Consumer Products Department along with Eugene?

(A) The Senior VP
(B) Jordan Jones
(C) Gary Shepherd
(D) Constance Hayes

Questions 7 through 9 refer to the following message.

WHILE YOU WERE OUT

To: *William Maxwell*
From: *Katherine Potter, Blade Travel*
Date: *Wed., February 2nd*
Time: *7:30 p.m.*

RETURNED YOUR CALL/ IMPORTANT/ <u>WILL CALL AGAIN</u>/ PLEASE CALL

MESSAGE: The air portion of your trip has not yet been confirmed. Confirmation will probably come early tomorrow. However, all ground and hotel reservations have been confirmed for you and Joseph Hill. All confirmation numbers, tickets, etc. will be sent by messenger to Mr. Hill once everything is finalized.

TAKEN BY: *David Sales*

7. Why did Katherine Potter call?

(A) To confirm William Maxwell's flight reservation
(B) To inform William Maxwell that his flight is not confirmed
(C) To ask William Maxwell to call Mr. Hill
(D) To make a booking

8. Who will be traveling?

(A) Only David Sales
(B) David Sales and William Maxwell
(C) William Maxwell and Joseph Hill
(D) Joseph Hill and Katherine Potter

9. Where does Katherine Potter probably work?

(A) A messenger service
(B) A hotel
(C) An airline
(D) A travel agency

Questions 10 through 12 refer to the following form.

Darnley's Dairy

We would like to thank all our loyal customers for choosing Darnley's Dairy for all their dairy needs. In order to streamline our delivery service, and to ensure you continue to receive our products in tip-top condition, we are asking all customers to fill out the order form below. Your details will be entered into our new customer database, and we will use this information to serve you better. As always, there will be no charge for home delivery.
Thank you.

Name: _____

Street Address: _____

City: _____

Order	Quantity	How often	Day
Fat-free milk	1 carton	3 times a week	Mon, Wed & Fri
Low-fat milk			
Whole milk			
Organic milk			
Flavored milk:			
Chocolate			
Strawberry	1 carton	2 times a week	Sat and Sun

Payment method:
Cash   XX
Credit card

Please return this to your Darnley's Dairy milk deliverer.

10. What is the purpose of this form?

(A) To catch customers who haven't paid their bills
(B) To improve their delivery service
(C) To thank customers
(D) To reduce delivery times

11. How much does Darnley's charge for home delivery?

(A) $1 per item
(B) It doesn't say.
(C) Nothing
(D) It depends on the item.

12. How many varieties of milk can be ordered using this form?

(A) Six
(B) Five
(C) Four
(D) Three

Questions 13 through 16 refer to the following memorandum.

MEMORANDUM

To: All Employees
From: Sidney Flanders, Office Manager
Date: September 4
Re: Vacation Days

Since it is never too early to be prepared, I am requesting that all employees promptly submit to their departmental managers any requests for vacation days for the remainder of the year. As you know, the end of the year is our busiest time, and there is always the problem of having to schedule vacations and personal time off around the end-of-year holidays. This is the most popular time for vacations, apart from the summer months, and it takes a lot of time to coordinate. I will work with all departmental managers to see that all vacation requests are honored where possible, except in cases where it is anticipated that the temporary staff will not be able to cover the projected workload. Unfortunately, we will have to request that some employees (generally employees with little seniority) postpone their vacation plans until a more convenient time. Those of you who do not get your first choice of vacation this time round will be given priority next time. However, please note that this is still not a flat guarantee that you will get your choice, even then. I would like to ask that all requests be made to the appropriate offices before the end of the week. Thank you for your cooperation in this matter. Rest assured that I will do my very best to accommodate all wishes.

---

13. Who will be receiving vacation requests?

(A) The personnel secretary
(B) The office manager
(C) All employees
(D) Temporary employees

14. What is true for employees with more seniority?

(A) They will not need to make vacation requests.
(B) They may be asked to postpone their vacations.
(C) They will probably have their vacation requests honored.
(D) They will not receive this memorandum.

15. According to the memo, when should requests for vacation time be made?

(A) By the end of the day
(B) By the end of the week
(C) By the end of the month
(D) By the end of the year

16. According to the memo, what problem often occurs?

(A) Employees do not schedule enough vacation time.
(B) Vacation time is used too early in the year.
(C) Departmental managers often reject requests for time off.
(D) There is difficulty scheduling vacations at year's end.

Questions 17 through 20 refer to the following letter.

Taylor and Bryce, Attorneys-at-Law
13 Woodlawn Avenue
Albany, NY 11208

Polar Airlines, Inc.
P.O. Box 1660-100
Minneapolis, MN 55440

Dear Sir/Madam,

I received this free mileage coupon (attached) from your airline when I took a flight to San Francisco in March. Though I am currently not enrolled in the Polar Miles Program, having read about the various benefits on offer, I am interested in becoming a member and receiving the 10,000 bonus Polar Miles offered with the coupon. In addition, I would like to have the mileage of my recent flights on your airline (ticket copies attached) credited to my new Polar Miles account, if possible.

I'd also like to take this opportunity to let you know that I appreciate all you did for me last December when I traveled on your airline from Boston to Finland. It was the first time I had used your airline, and to be honest, I had my doubts about what kind of service to expect. However, I am happy to say that I was proven wrong. The plane was six hours late taking off (due to a terrible Christmas Eve blizzard—over which I know you had little control!), but your staff did all they could to ameliorate the situation. I plan to continue to fly your airline because of the courteous assistance and service I received from Polar Airlines employees during that long delay and subsequent flight.

Yours sincerely,

Anthony Taylor

17. What was Mr. Taylor's reason for writing to Polar Airlines?

(A) He wanted to make a complaint.
(B) He wanted to enroll in an air miles program.
(C) He wanted to make a reservation.
(D) He wanted to apply for a job.

18. What did Mr. Taylor receive from Polar Airlines in March?

(A) A coupon
(B) His Polar Miles membership
(C) 10,000 Polar Miles
(D) Courteous service

19. Where is this letter being sent from?

(A) Finland
(B) Minneapolis
(C) Albany
(D) Boston

20. What caused Mr. Taylor's plane to be delayed?

(A) Lack of assistance
(B) Weather conditions
(C) Mechanical problems
(D) Poor control by Polar Airlines

Questions 21 through 24 refer to the following letter.

Dear Alberta Bank Customer,

The following contains important information about your new Alberta Bank ATM/Debit card. Please read it carefully. This information could help protect you against fraudulent use of your card by others.

Instructions regarding the enclosed item(s):

- If the enclosed Alberta Bank Card replaces a valid card that is about to expire, simply sign the back of the new card and begin using it as you would ordinarily. Your confidential Personal Identification Number (PIN) is the same one you have been using.
- In all other cases, please take it to the Alberta Bank branch which is most convenient for you to sign and validate your new Bank Card, and choose a new PIN. The Alberta Bank recommends that customers do not use dates of birth as their PIN. Please remember to bring two forms of identification with you, such as a passport, student ID card, driver's license, or credit card issued by the Alberta Bank.

If your Bank Card is lost, stolen or damaged, please call the Alberta Bank Card Helpline, in operation 24 hours a day. The telephone number for this helpline can be found on the back of your card. We advise you to make a note of this and keep it in a safe place. Remember, please destroy your old bank card properly.

Do not hesitate to visit any of our branches any time you have any questions about the Alberta Bank and our wide range of services.

Sincerely,

Alberta Bank

---

21. What was enclosed with this letter?

(A) A Personal Identification Number
(B) A new Bank Card
(C) A bank statement
(D) An expiration notice

22. Who is the letter from?

(A) Friends
(B) A customer
(C) A bank
(D) An advertising agency

23. If this card is a replacement for a lost card, what must the customer do?

(A) Begin using the card as usual
(B) Call Alberta Bank
(C) Visit an Alberta Bank branch
(D) Pick up a new card

24. Which of the following is NOT recommended as a PIN?

(A) Customer's favorite numbers
(B) Customer's date of birth
(C) Dates from US history
(D) Binary numbers

Questions 25 through 28 refer to the following fax.

To: Celia Kelly
From: Andrew Mathers
Date: Saturday, March 21
Re: Arrival in Tokyo

   I have been unexpectedly called to an emergency meeting in Seoul this weekend, and thus will not be able to meet Mr. Robert Bayer at Narita Airport in Tokyo tomorrow morning (Sunday, March 22) as planned. I'm sorry not to have contacted you earlier about this, but the call came through just as I was about to board my flight to Japan from New York.

   I was fortunate enough to get a seat right away on a plane for Seoul, so instead of being on my way to Tokyo right now, I am currently waiting in San Francisco to embark on the final leg of my flight to Korea.

   This whole thing was quite unforeseen, and I apologize for any inconvenience it may have caused; however, my presence in Seoul this weekend is urgently needed. I will contact you again upon my arrival there. My business in Korea will be concluded by Monday afternoon, so I expect no difficulty in being present for the start of the Tokyo conference on Tuesday morning. My assistant, Ms. Alice Lang, will be arriving there as planned, and will act as my agent until my arrival. I have asked her to contact Mr. Bayer as soon as possible to explain the situation and then to meet with him on my behalf according to our original schedule. I have no doubt Ms. Lang will handle the situation professionally and diplomatically.

25. Who will be meeting in Tokyo on Sunday?

(A) Alice Lang and Robert Bayer
(B) Celia Kelly and Robert Bayer
(C) Andrew Mathers and Alice Lang
(D) Celia Kelly and Andrew Mathers

26. Who will be the last person informed of the change of plans?

(A) Alice Lang
(B) Celia Kelly
(C) Robert Bayer
(D) Andrew Mathers

27. Where will Andrew Mathers most likely be on Tuesday morning?

(A) San Francisco
(B) Tokyo
(C) Seoul
(D) New York

28. Due to which of the following reasons is Andrew Mathers changing his plans?

(A) He decided to take a last minute vacation.
(B) He has to attend an emergency meeting.
(C) He didn't want to meet Robert Bayer.
(D) He thinks Alice Lang can do a better job.

Questions 29 through 33 refer to the following chart and memo.

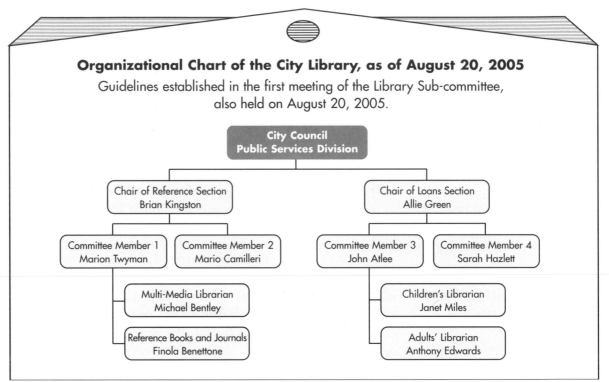

Organizational Chart of the City Library, as of August 20, 2005

Guidelines established in the first meeting of the Library Sub-committee, also held on August 20, 2005.

MEMO

To: All members of the City Library Sub-committee and Library employees
From: Alex Farino, City Council Director of Public Services
Re: Organizational Hierarchy
Date: September 12, 2005

Please take a look at the attached chart. As you know, the City Library sub-committee was set up to deal with the day-to-day running of the city library, and as an effort to improve the overall efficiency of this institution. At the inaugural meeting on August 20th, the official chain of command, so to speak, was established. However, it seems that the primary reason for the existence of the committee has been misunderstood by the majority of the members. I have been receiving individual documents and letters from most of the people named on the chart. The whole purpose of making this chart was to prevent this from happening. All complaints and problems regarding the reference and multi-media sections of the library should be reported by the librarians in charge to committee members 1 or 2. After discussion, if they are unable to resolve the complaint, then they should take it to the next level, in other words, to the chairman of the Reference Section, Brian Kingston. Should he feel it necessary, he may bring matters to my attention; otherwise, he is authorized to take action as he sees fit. It is the same scenario with the adults' and children's lending libraries: first approach committee members 3 or 4, who will then approach the relevant chairperson if needed. Under no circumstances should anyone approach me directly. I urge you to follow this protocol.

29. What is the name of the person at the top of the chart?

 (A) City Council
 (B) Brian Kingston
 (C) Allie Green
 (D) Alex Farino

30. What is the purpose of this memo?

 (A) To remind members of the next meeting
 (B) To remind members of whom to contact about problems
 (C) To explain the library sections
 (D) To thank the members of the library sub-committee

31. Who is in charge of books for library users under 10 years of age?

 (A) Finola Benettone
 (B) Anthony Edwards
 (C) John Atlee
 (D) Janet Miles

32. Whom should Anthony Edwards contact if he has a problem?

 (A) Janet Miles
 (B) John Atlee or Sarah Hazlett
 (C) Allie Green or Brian Kingston
 (D) Michael Bentley

33. Has the new organization of the library been a success?

 (A) Yes, overall, but with some minor difficulties.
 (B) It does not say.
 (C) No, the members have ignored the chain of command.
 (D) Yes, it is a great success.

Questions 34 through 38 refer to the following schedule and fax.

Flight #	Departure time	Arrival time	Destination	Notes
ALA222	23:05 May 2nd	06:30 May 3rd	Pisa	1 Aisle seat 1 Kosher meal
ALA223	15:50 May 5th	10:00 May 6th	Tokyo	1 Aisle seat 1 Kosher meal

May 3rd
06:30 Arrival at airport — pick-up by representative from Ferrari
10:30 Meeting with car interiors design team
12:00 Lunch
13:00 Tour of factory
15:00 Meeting with Chief Engineers
16:30 Your presentation (to Board of Directors)
19:00 Dinner with members of the Board of Directors

May 4th
08:00 Breakfast meeting with Paolo Svegli
09:15 Tour of second factory site
11:30 Meeting with Maria Modesta
13:00 Lunch — free time
16:00 Your second presentation (to export division)
19:00 Dinner reception

May 5th
A.M. Free time (9:00-13:00 sightseeing — individual tour arranged)
13:30 check in for flight. Tour guide will accompany you to airport.

Hotel reservation: 2 nights, single room at the Astoria

MEMO

To: Alistair Black
Fax #: 023-999-9998
From: Wendy Hartwell (Travel)
Fax #: 023-998-9998

Dear Mr. Black,

As requested, I am sending you a detailed itinerary for your forthcoming trip to Italy. As you will see, both your outgoing and return flights have been confirmed, and I have reserved an aisle seat both ways. I have been in direct contact with our Pisa branch, and they have obtained the schedule of meetings and events planned for your stay in Italy. We have succeeded in arranging a brief meeting with Mr. Paolo Svegli of the Italian Motor Vehicle Manufacturers Association, although he is willing to give no more than 1 hour of his time. I know that you have already been in touch with him by email, so I think that this should be long enough to discuss your proposal in person. If he is interested enough to set up this initial meeting, I think we may have a good chance of setting up the contract.

You'll have one morning of sightseeing before you leave. The guide will take you directly to the airport. Don't hesitate to get in touch if you have any questions.

Have a good trip.

Regards
Wendy Hartwell.

34. What is probably the purpose of Alistair Black's trip?

(A) To set up a contract with an Italian motor manufacturer

(B) To set up a new factory

(C) To have an aisle seat

(D) To fly to Tokyo

35. To whom will Alistair Black be making presentations?

(A) Maria Modesta

(B) The Board of Directors and the Export Division

(C) Paolo Svegli and the Chief Engineers

(D) Employees at two factories

36. Which of the following statements is probably NOT true?

(A) Alistair Black has been communicating with Paolo Svegli.

(B) Alistair Black is good friends with Paolo Svegli.

(C) Paolo Svegli has little spare time to meet with Alistair Black.

(D) Alistair Black has Paolo Svegli's email address.

37. Whom will Mr. Black probably be traveling with?

(A) With a business associate

(B) With his spouse

(C) No one

(D) Paolo Svegli

38. How long will Mr. Black spend sightseeing?

(A) One full day

(B) No time during this trip

(C) Several hours

(D) 3 days and 2 nights

Questions 39 through 43 refer to the following agenda and memo.

Agenda

Personnel Department Monthly Meeting
Monday 14th July, 4:30 p.m.
Interview Room 3

New Business
- Appointment of new department head
- Relocation — new office sites
- New policy on interviewing
- New employee health insurance system

Reports
- Interviewer training committee
- Employee relations workshop

Other business
(please notify me by July 10th if you have other items to add)

MEMO

To: All Personnel Department employees
From: Ursula
Date: July 2nd
Re: Meeting agenda

This is a quick reminder about this month's meeting, which will be held a week earlier than usual. This is because the third Monday this month is a national holiday, and all offices will be closed. Be sure to make a note of this date because absences will not be excused. In addition, please note the change of location. It will be held in interview room 3 this time, not room 2 because of complaints about the broken air conditioner. The management has decided not to fix the air conditioning because we will be relocating around the middle of August. The new location of our office is item number 3 on the agenda. Please bring any ideas you have on facilities that you feel should be provided in our new location. I will be handing out forms at the meeting for you to fill in with your ideas. There will be an explanation of our new employee health insurance system. Mark Southwold will be explaining how the new system will save you money, while increasing overall coverage. He has asked me to inform you that he is willing to talk one on one with anyone interested, but please make an appointment with his secretary first.

Because we have a lot of important things to discuss, I foresee the meeting running a little longer than usual, so please be sure to arrive on time.

39. Why is the meeting earlier than usual?

(A) The regular meeting day will be a day off this month.

(B) The regular time is being moved from Mondays.

(C) There was no meeting last month.

(D) The company felt that it was time for a change.

40. What would have been the date of the meeting if it had not been changed?

(A) Seven days early

(B) July 21st

(C) Monday

(D) July 28th

41. Why isn't the management going to repair the air conditioning?

(A) It is too expensive.

(B) The weather is cooler these days.

(C) The company will move to another building.

(D) They are waiting for permission.

42. Who should notify Ursula by July 10th?

(A) People who will be absent from the meeting

(B) People who want to consult Mark Southwold

(C) People who want to add items to the agenda

(D) People who wish to attend the meeting

43. Which of the following statements is NOT true?

(A) The department is changing its interview policy.

(B) The personnel department will have a new head.

(C) The new insurance system is costlier than the old one.

(D) The department has at least three interview rooms.

Questions 44 through 48 refer to the following emails.

Dear Nancy,

Thank you for getting back to me so quickly. I haven't forgotten what we discussed, and I will be having a meeting with Bob Jones later this afternoon. Do you want me to ask him if the budget can be raised to $350,000? We had set a budget of $300,000, but after going through the building plans with you and the architect, I think that it is not going to be enough. I have been going through the books, and I think the firm can manage it. I am pretty sure that, together, you and I can come up with a pretty persuasive package that we can take to the next level if Bob is unwilling to discuss it today. I know that he is the person I am supposed to consult first, but frankly, he lacks the power to make that kind of decision.
Let me know what you think.

Anita

Dear Anita,

Well, I too have been looking at the figures, and I think that maybe we should ask for $400,000. It is embarrassing to go way over budget once a project has begun, so I would rather ask for more before we begin and not have to cut corners later. I think it is a waste of time going over everything with Bob, but I understand that this is the procedure. Talk to him so that he knows what is going on, but make an appointment to talk to Joseph Green, too. He is a lot more influential, and I know that he has been interested in this project from the start. It will definitely help to have him on our side. See if you can get Rosemary Connors to come along, too—let's make a mini-presentation to them both. If they both like our ideas, I think we will have no trouble getting what we want.

Talk to you later,
Nancy

44. What are Anita and Nancy trying to do?

(A) Stop Bob Jones from attending a meeting

(B) Gain extra funding for a project

(C) Make dinner plans

(D) Meet influential people

45. How much does Nancy want the budget raised?

(A) Half as much as Anita

(B) By a third

(C) By $50,000

(D) An unspecified amount

46. Whom does Nancy want to make a presentation to?

(A) Bob Jones

(B) Bob Jones and Joseph Green

(C) Joseph Green and Rosemary Connors

(D) Rosemary Connors, Joseph Green and Bob Jones

47. What kind of project are Anita and Nancy probably working on?

(A) Construction of a building

(B) Decorating a house

(C) Starting their own company

(D) Investing in the stock market

48. Among the following, who probably holds the highest position?

(A) Nancy

(B) Anita

(C) Bob Jones

(D) Joseph Green

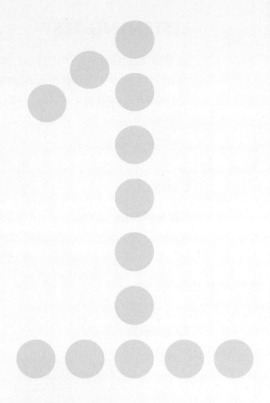

PRACTICE TEST

General Directions

This test is designed to measure your language ability.
The test is divided into two sections: Listening and Reading.

You must mark all of your answers on the separate answer sheet.
For each question, you should select the best answer from the answer choices given. Then, on your answer sheet, you should find the number of the question and fill in the space that corresponds to the letter of the answer that you have selected. If you decide to change an answer, completely erase your old answer and then mark your new answer.

LISTENING TEST

In the Listening test, you will be asked to demonstrate how well you understand spoken English. The entire Listening section of the test will last approximately 45 minutes. Directions are given for each of the four parts. There is a separate answer sheet for marking answers. Do not write your answers in the test book.

Part 1

Directions: In this part of the test, you will hear four statements about each picture in your textbook. After listening to all four statements, you must select the one statement that best describes what you see in the picture. Then find the number of that question on your answer sheet and mark your answer. The statements will be spoken only one time, and are not printed in your test book.

Sample Answer

Example

Now listen to the four statements.

Statement (B), "The woman is typing on a computer," best describes what you see in the picture. Therefore, you should choose answer (B).

1.

2.

Go on to the next page.

3.

4.

5.

6.

Go on to the next page.

7.

8.

9.

10.

Go on to the next page.

Part 2

Directions: In this section you will hear a question or statement followed by three responses. Select the best response to the question or statement and mark the letter (A), (B), or (C) on your answer sheet. Again, each response will be spoken only one time and will not be printed in your test book.

Example

You will hear: How are you today?

You will also hear: (A) I'm fine, thank you.
                     (B) It's cold, isn't it?
                     (C) Well, it's a difficult issue.

The best response to the question "How are you today?" is choice (A), "I'm fine, thank you." Therefore, you should choose answer (A).

11. Mark your answer on your answer sheet.

12. Mark your answer on your answer sheet.

13. Mark your answer on your answer sheet.

14. Mark your answer on your answer sheet.

15. Mark your answer on your answer sheet.

16. Mark your answer on your answer sheet.

17. Mark your answer on your answer sheet.

18. Mark your answer on your answer sheet.

19. Mark your answer on your answer sheet.

20. Mark your answer on your answer sheet.

21. Mark your answer on your answer sheet.

22. Mark your answer on your answer sheet.

23. Mark your answer on your answer sheet.

24. Mark your answer on your answer sheet.

25. Mark your answer on your answer sheet.

26. Mark your answer on your answer sheet.

27. Mark your answer on your answer sheet.

28. Mark your answer on your answer sheet.

29. Mark your answer on your answer sheet.

30. Mark your answer on your answer sheet.

31. Mark your answer on your answer sheet.

32. Mark your answer on your answer sheet.

33. Mark your answer on your answer sheet.

34. Mark your answer on your answer sheet.

35. Mark your answer on your answer sheet.

36. Mark your answer on your answer sheet.

37. Mark your answer on your answer sheet.

38. Mark your answer on your answer sheet.

39. Mark your answer on your answer sheet.

40. Mark your answer on your answer sheet.

Part 3

Directions: In this section of the test, you will hear a number of conversations between two people. You will be asked to answer three questions about what is said in each conversation. You must select the best response to each question and mark the letter (A), (B), (C), or (D) on your answer sheet. Each conversation will be spoken only one time and will not be printed in your test book.

41. What was the man waiting for?

    (A) The woman
    (B) A shipment of material
    (C) An appointment
    (D) A sale at a department store

42. Who has been calling every day?

    (A) The customs officials
    (B) The department store
    (C) The woman's mother
    (D) Nobody

43. Why did it take so long?

    (A) The company forgot to send the package.
    (B) There was a mistake in the address.
    (C) It was held up at customs.
    (D) The woman forgot to give it to the man.

44. What is the man doing?

    (A) Taking a week's vacation
    (B) Trying to repair a computer
    (C) Making photocopies
    (D) Making a phone call

45. Why is the woman surprised?

    (A) She thought the man had quit.
    (B) She heard that he had given up.
    (C) The man was very rude to her.
    (D) The man has been doing the same task for a week.

46. When does the man expect to finish?

    (A) He won't. It's too complicated.
    (B) Sometime next week
    (C) Before the end of the day
    (D) Tomorrow

Go on to the next page.

47. What is the woman's problem?

   (A) She doesn't have enough cash on her.
   (B) She has lost her check book.
   (C) She can't find her credit card.
   (D) She can't find her wallet.

48. How does the woman want to pay?

   (A) By credit card
   (B) By debit card
   (C) By check
   (D) By cash on delivery

49. What does the woman need to show the clerk?

   (A) Her address
   (B) Two forms of identification
   (C) One form of identification
   (D) Her check book

50. According to the woman, what is special about tomorrow?

   (A) It's her birthday.
   (B) It's the man's birthday.
   (C) It's a national holiday.
   (D) It's Friday.

51. Why will the man go to work?

   (A) He doesn't like holidays.
   (B) It will be nice and quiet in the office.
   (C) He hates birthdays.
   (D) He has a lot of work to catch up on.

52. What is the woman going to do tomorrow?

   (A) She plans to come to the office, too.
   (B) She hopes to sort out orders.
   (C) She will enjoy having a day off.
   (D) She doesn't say.

53. Why is the man worried?

    (A) He thinks he'll be late for work.
    (B) He thinks his boss dislikes him.
    (C) He thinks the woman will be late.
    (D) He expects trouble in the stock market.

54. How long does he have to get to work?

    (A) One hour
    (B) Thirty minutes
    (C) One hour and thirty minutes
    (D) As long as he wants

55. What does the woman think?

    (A) He'll get into a lot of trouble.
    (B) He'll probably lose his job.
    (C) He'll get there in time.
    (D) He should take a taxi.

---

56. What is the man looking for?

    (A) A telephone
    (B) A new battery
    (C) A store
    (D) Directions

57. Which store has a broken payphone?

    (A) The store next door
    (B) The store the man is in currently
    (C) Both this store and the store next door
    (D) Neither store

58. What does the woman say about her cell phone?

    (A) The battery is dead.
    (B) The man can borrow it if he wants.
    (C) She never lends it to customers.
    (D) She doesn't have one.

Go on to the next page.

59. Where does the man live?

    (A) Near the office
    (B) A couple of blocks from work
    (C) Near the subway station
    (D) Near the woman

60. Who brings the woman to work three days a week?

    (A) The man
    (B) Her brother
    (C) Her husband
    (D) Her sister

61. Why doesn't the woman take the subway?

    (A) The bus is cheaper.
    (B) The bus is easier to take.
    (C) The subway is far from her home.
    (D) She dislikes the subway.

---

62. Where is the man going?

    (A) Home
    (B) To have a coffee with John
    (C) To John's office
    (D) To a meeting

63. Why can't the woman go with them?

    (A) She is allergic to coffee.
    (B) She has to attend a meeting.
    (C) She is waiting on a phone call.
    (D) She has a lunch appointment.

64. Which of the following does the woman want?

    (A) A large coffee and a sandwich
    (B) A large coffee only
    (C) A large coffee and a banana muffin
    (D) A large coffee and a blueberry muffin

65. What are the man and woman discussing?

    (A) Their vacation in Singapore
    (B) Designs for a new building
    (C) Shipping costs
    (D) A meeting they both attended

66. Why will Amy and Hank have to make some changes?

    (A) There are some mistakes in the structure of the building.
    (B) The Tanaka Corporation doesn't like the design.
    (C) They forgot to label the diagrams.
    (D) There are no changes needed.

67. What kind of company do the man and woman probably work for?

    (A) A shipping company
    (B) A fashion design company
    (C) An architectural firm
    (D) A post office

---

68. What has the man heard about the personnel department?

    (A) There will be major changes made to the personnel department.
    (B) The company is expanding the personnel department.
    (C) He is going to be promoted to head of the personnel department.
    (D) The personnel department will hire several new workers.

69. According to the woman, why is the personnel manager leaving?

    (A) He is not leaving.
    (B) He is taking early retirement.
    (C) He is taking sick leave.
    (D) He was offered a better job elsewhere.

70. What is the woman's opinion of the man?

    (A) He is a hardworking employee.
    (B) He pays too much attention to idle gossip.
    (C) He needs to find a new job.
    (D) He has been getting slack lately.

Go on to the next page.

Part 4

Directions: In this section of the test, you will hear a number of short talks given by a single speaker. Again, you must answer three questions about what is said in each talk. Choose the most appropriate response to each question and mark the letter (A), (B), (C), or (D) on your answer sheet. Each talk will be spoken only one time and will not be printed in your test book.

71. Who is Carol Draper?

    (A) A popular novelist
    (B) A magazine editor
    (C) An investment banker
    (D) A famous politician

72. How long has Carol Draper held her current position?

    (A) 6 months
    (B) 1 year
    (C) 2 years
    (D) This evening

73. What will Carol Draper do after her speech?

    (A) She will answer questions.
    (B) She will sign her book.
    (C) She will have dinner.
    (D) She will show a film.

74. What type of business is Eagle?

    (A) An airline
    (B) A travel agency
    (C) A car rental company
    (D) A large hotel chain

75. According to the message, how can one obtain rate information?

    (A) Call another number
    (B) Leave a message
    (C) Send an email
    (D) Visit another location

76. Which of the following times is the office NOT open?

    (A) Monday 7:30 a.m.
    (B) Friday 4:30 p.m.
    (C) Sunday 6:30 p.m.
    (D) Wednesday 10:00 p.m.

77. What happens at 9:00 p.m.?

    (A) The whole library will close.
    (B) The children's section closes.
    (C) Normal operations resume.
    (D) Parents must meet their children.

78. Why is a section of the library being closed early?

    (A) There is a medical emergency.
    (B) There is a maintenance problem.
    (C) It rarely closes at 9:00 p.m.
    (D) It is closing early in order to reopen tomorrow.

79. What advice is given to people planning to bring children to the library tomorrow?

    (A) Do not bring children tomorrow
    (B) Leave immediately
    (C) Telephone first
    (D) Send a fax

---

80. What is being specially discounted?

    (A) Children's toys
    (B) Flashlights
    (C) Batteries
    (D) Smoke detectors

81. When are the special prices in effect?

    (A) While the light is flashing
    (B) Twenty-five minutes each day
    (C) For the next 40 minutes
    (D) Every day this week

82. What sizes are being discounted?

    (A) All sizes
    (B) Small
    (C) Small and medium
    (D) Large

Go on to the next page.

83. How often does the radio station have a weather report?

(A) Once an hour
(B) 12 times a day
(C) Twice a day
(D) Once a day

84. What is happening in the western mountains?

(A) People have been injured.
(B) There have been tornados.
(C) There are accidents on the highways.
(D) Heavy rain continues to fall.

85. What happened to dozens of people in the South?

(A) They were injured.
(B) They were killed.
(C) They were kept off the highway.
(D) They were trapped for 12 hours.

---

86. Who are Jim and Tammy?

(A) Country music singers
(B) Contest finalists
(C) Radio show hosts
(D) Paula Chen's friends

87. What is Paula Chen told to do?

(A) Request some country music
(B) Phone the radio station
(C) Win $10,000
(D) Collect her prize

88. What will happen if Paula Chen doesn't do what is mentioned?

(A) She will lose her job.
(B) She will win a prize.
(C) She will lose the chance to win some money.
(D) She will make Jim and Tammy angry.

89. Who is being held at the airport?

    (A) Customs officials
    (B) News reporters
    (C) Five suspects
    (D) Confidential sources

90. Why are they being held?

    (A) For carrying false passports
    (B) For drug smuggling
    (C) For diplomatic reasons
    (D) To return to San Lorenzo

91. What is the lightest punishment if they are found guilty in this case?

    (A) 25 years in prison
    (B) A $25,000 fine
    (C) Loss of their passports
    (D) 2 years imprisonment

---

92. Who is this announcement intended for?

    (A) New employees
    (B) The driver of a truck
    (C) Store customers
    (D) The tow truck owner

93. What will happen if the truck is not moved?

    (A) The owner will be fired.
    (B) It will be towed off.
    (C) The loading ramp will be used.
    (D) The truck may be damaged.

94. Where should the driver have parked instead?

    (A) In a parking lot behind the plant
    (B) In a parking lot across the street
    (C) In the town center
    (D) In the loading bay

Go on to the next page.

95. What is true of the Capital Express?

    (A) It is the fastest train in the world.
    (B) Tickets for it are very expensive.
    (C) It operates in North America.
    (D) It travels throughout the country.

96. How long is the trip to Washington on the Capital Express?

    (A) Nearly 105 miles
    (B) About 175 kilometers
    (C) Around three hours
    (D) Over six hours

97. What kind of service is available on the train?

    (A) A massage service
    (B) A food and beverage service
    (C) A book-lending service
    (D) A priority ticket reservation service

---

98. Who is Larry?

    (A) A high-school student
    (B) The woman's son
    (C) A houseguest
    (D) The woman's nephew

99. What is available for Larry to eat for dinner?

    (A) A pizza, vegetables, and ice cream
    (B) A salad and ice cream
    (C) A hamburger and fries
    (D) Ice cream and cake

100. When is Larry supposed to do his homework?

    (A) Before he eats his dinner
    (B) After he has a pizza
    (C) Before eight o'clock
    (D) When the woman comes home

This is the end of the Listening test. Turn to Part 5 in your test book.

READING TEST

In the Reading test, you will be required to answer several types of reading comprehension questions based on a variety of texts. The Reading section of the test will last approximately 75 minutes. There are three parts, and directions are given for each part. You are encouraged to answer as many questions as possible within the time allowed.

You must mark your answers on the separate answer sheet. Do not write your answers in the test book.

Part 5

Directions: In each question, you will find a word or phrase missing. Four answer choices are given below each sentence. You must choose the best answer to complete the sentence. Then mark the letter (A), (B), (C), or (D) on your answer sheet.

101. Today's deposits total $4,800.00, leaving you with a balance ------- $10,665.62.
   (A) to
   (B) of
   (C) for
   (D) from

102. I called her on at least three occasions, but she ------- got back to me.
   (A) rarely
   (B) sometimes
   (C) never
   (D) usually

103. We ------- to inform you that your application for credit has been disapproved.
   (A) revert
   (B) resent
   (C) regret
   (D) reject

104. Six months -------, construction was begun on the hospital's new wing.
   (A) ago
   (B) then
   (C) since
   (D) before

Go on to the next page.

105. This is a restricted area; entry by ------- personnel is strictly forbidden.

(A) unauthorized
(B) exclusive
(C) impertinent
(D) declassified

106. The 30 extra books were ------- on top of a desk in an unused office.

(A) restored
(B) arraigned
(C) ordered
(D) stacked

107. ------- you not spoken up like that, the issue would probably never have been addressed.

(A) Did
(B) Should
(C) Are
(D) Had

108. Employers ------- to pay their employees a decent wage.

(A) must
(B) ought
(C) should
(D) would

109. The board voted to ------- the chairman, whose tenure had been marked by ever-increasing losses.

(A) fete
(B) oust
(C) jeer
(D) cede

110. One worry is that higher tax rates will cause a slowing of the economy, which will in turn lead to a decrease, rather than an increase, in tax -------.

(A) ratios
(B) revenue
(C) regulation
(D) allotment

111. ------- many others who lost money investing in its stock, Green wanted to see criminal charges brought against Seleron Corporation officials.

    (A) As
    (B) Like
    (C) Because
    (D) Although

112. The managing director asked his ------- to contact the shareholders regarding the crisis management meeting.

    (A) aid
    (B) aide
    (C) aided
    (D) addition

113. ------- all of the newly-hired employees were unhappy with the organization of the orientation schedule.

    (A) Most
    (B) Mostly
    (C) Almost
    (D) Every

114. Customers wishing to make complaints ------- ask to talk to one of our customer service consultants, who will be pleased to help them.

    (A) should
    (B) might
    (C) ought
    (D) had

115. If Mr. Singh ------- to apply for the position, he would be hired in an instant.

    (A) may
    (B) were
    (C) is
    (D) will

116. The investigating committee announced that it would put ------- releasing its findings for at least another week.

    (A) off
    (B) upon
    (C) down
    (D) up

Go on to the next page.

117. Janet was understandably quite nervous, never ------- spoken in front of such a large crowd before.

(A) has
(B) had
(C) have
(D) having

118. The interviewer ------- to, but never mentioned outright, the rumors of internal dissention.

(A) conferred
(B) deferred
(C) alluded
(D) secluded

119. The company's accountants tried to ------- nearly $1,000,000 in earnings so as to avoid paying taxes on it.

(A) dismiss
(B) reveal
(C) remiss
(D) conceal

120. We need to sell this in a hurry, so we are going to take ------- the first buyer offers for it.

(A) whatever
(B) however
(C) whomever
(D) whoever

121. ------- anyone listening to the speech understood its eventual importance.

(A) Nearly
(B) Hardly
(C) Fairly
(D) Actually

122. Her speech did not inspire any public support; -------, it made people less sympathetic to her cause.

(A) although
(B) otherwise
(C) indeed
(D) factually

123. Experts advise that a speaker ------- both alone and in front of a live audience prior to delivering a major address.

    (A) retell
    (B) revoke
    (C) restate
    (D) rehearse

124. Marion Smith of Merston Enterprises has asked me to make this presentation here today, on ------- behalf.

    (A) theirs
    (B) my
    (C) her
    (D) hers

125. Planning the new office layout has been the hardest task I ------- in a long while.

    (A) had have
    (B) did have
    (C) did had
    (D) have had

126. Fortunately, changing the members of the committee halfway through the project has had no noticeable ------- on the price of shares.

    (A) point
    (B) affectation
    (C) affect
    (D) effect

127. I want you to instruct the movers to put all of the boxes in the largest room ------- the first floor.

    (A) on
    (B) in
    (C) to
    (D) for

128. Everyone ------- been wonderful to work with, and I will sorely miss working here.

    (A) have
    (B) did
    (C) hasn't
    (D) has

Go on to the next page.

129. Sandra is incredibly ------- in everything she does. She was given an award for her quick work last year.

(A) efficient
(B) effortless
(C) affluent
(D) affective

130. The committee ------- that we do not pursue legal action at this time, but wait for the result of the tests.

(A) suggesting
(B) is recommending
(C) has
(D) is recommended

131. The management has agreed not to take further action, ------- you do not commit any further violations of company policy.

(A) granted
(B) therefore
(C) provided
(D) moreover

132. I ------- never have hired him if his references had given me any indication of how unreliable he would be.

(A) would
(B) will
(C) must
(D) had

133. I will be announcing to the media today that all ------- from sales of this CD will go to charity.

(A) proceeds
(B) precedes
(C) precedent
(D) results

134. A new branch of that coffee shop chain will be opening in the shopping center ------- Friday morning.

(A) in
(B) to
(C) on
(D) off

135. According to Nancy in the quality control department, there have been ------- customer complaints this month. This is a great improvement on the preceding two months.

    (A) few
    (B) a few
    (C) some
    (D) none

136. It is imperative that quality is not sacrificed for profits. We have ------- the best products at the best prices.

    (A) provide
    (B) to be providing
    (C) to provide
    (D) profited

137. The worst that can happen ------- that the store will have to alter its operating hours until we can hire replacement staff.

    (A) are
    (B) was
    (C) is
    (D) have

138. The finance office is unable to ------- reimbursements unless all pertinent receipts are submitted.

    (A) approve
    (B) make approvals
    (C) approve of
    (D) appropriate

139. I ------- insist on a revision of next year's budget by Friday. It must be ready before the annual general meeting at the end of the month.

    (A) could
    (B) must
    (C) may
    (D) have

140. There has been a leak of confidential data to one of our biggest -------. It would seem that we are the victims of corporate espionage.

    (A) enemies
    (B) oppositions
    (C) rivals
    (D) opposites

Go on to the next page.

Part 6

Directions: Read the texts on the following pages. You will find a word or phrase missing in some of the sentences. Below each of the sentences, four answer choices are given. Select the most appropriate answer to complete the text. Then mark the letter (A), (B), (C), or (D) on your answer sheet.

Dear Mrs. Whitman,

I regret to inform you that your application for a government subsidized housing ------- has been

141. (A) permission
(B) loan
(C) affirmation
(D) agree

rejected. While we understand that you recently became unemployed, as a home owner who has more than $10,000 dollars currently ------- in a bank account, you simply do not fit any of the basic

142. (A) withdrawn
(B) transfer
(C) deposited
(D) mortgage

criteria for a subsidized housing loan. However, as a single parent, if you are receiving no financial support from the father of your children, you may qualify for child care assistance. I suggest that you contact our office to make an appointment to discuss this further. The number to call for -------

143. (A) denomination
(B) consultation
(C) remittance
(D) talking

appointments is 023-445-4460. The phone line is operational between the hours of 9:00 a.m. and 6:00 p.m. Please have your social security number on hand when you call. This ------- speed up the process.

144. (A) is helping
(B) helped
(C) will help
(D) used to help

Sincerely,

Clarence Dewitt

Go on to the next page.

Over the last few months, we have received ------- letters from readers, asking us where they can

145. (A) much
(B) a lot of
(C) numbers of
(D) lots

buy some of the items that have been on display in the background of a number of our fashion features. It almost seems that the furnishings and decorative items from those photo shoots have ------- interest than the clothes themselves.

146. (A) aroused more
(B) aroused
(C) provoked
(D) made more

For this reason you will notice that, starting on page 78 of this month's edition, we have introduced a new feature entitled "Where can I buy...?" This new section will appear immediately after our main fashion photo feature each month. We will be listing the designers and manufacturers for just about everything you can see in each photo, and we will be giving you the numbers and websites you need to find out more. Many of these items will be made available at a ------- to magazine subscribers.

147. (A) bargain
(B) price off
(C) major retailer
(D) discount

All the more reason to take out a subscription!
Take a ------- and let us know what you think.

148. (A) break
(B) time
(C) off
(D) look

Questions 149 through 152 refer to the following message.

To: Fiona Kim
From: Baljit Singh
Subject: Urgent Business

Ms. Kim:

I wish you to present yourself at my office at 9:00 a.m. tomorrow. It has been ------- to my attention by

149. (A) made
     (B) presented
     (C) brought
     (D) held

various members of staff that you have not been acting in a very cooperative manner of late, and I feel we need to meet to discuss the -------. I was very surprised to hear this, and although I have

150. (A) circumstance
     (B) situation
     (C) development
     (D) event

been ignoring it, hoping that this was a temporary matter, it has been going on long enough that I think we need to talk.

I will not go into ------- in this memo, but needless to say we will be discussing three major incidents

151. (A) details
     (B) information
     (C) carefully
     (D) in detail

which have caused us to lose important contracts. I have not yet decided what will happen to your position at this company; it depends rather on the outcome of our meeting tomorrow and the outcome of a second meeting that I will have with both of your ------- tomorrow afternoon.

152. (A) watchers
     (B) foreman
     (C) leaders
     (D) supervisors

Go on to the next page.

Part 7

Directions: In this part of the test, you will read a selection of texts, such as magazine and newspaper articles, letters, and advertisements. Each text is followed by several questions. Choose the correct answer to each question and mark the letter (A), (B), (C), or (D) on your answer sheet.

FAX

To: John Andersen, Andersen Components
From: Max Green, Herbert Rails
Re: Cancellation of order
Date: March 23[rd,]

Dear John,
I have bad news, I'm afraid. We are going to have to cancel the order for the 5000 m of electric cables, 5000 nuts and bolts, and the 50 bolt cutters which was placed yesterday morning. We had expected to be awarded a contract to lay rails for a new private railway, but at the last minute, they gave the contract to someone else. Sorry for the inconvenience.

Sincerely,

Max

---

153. What is the purpose of this fax?

(A) To place an order
(B) To cancel an order
(C) To confirm an order
(D) To ask for advice

154. What had Herbert Rails expected to receive?

(A) A contract to work for a private railway
(B) 5000 m of electric cables
(C) Some bad news
(D) A reward

155. Which of the following can be inferred from the fax?

(A) Max Green has never contacted John Andersen before.
(B) Max Green is interested in computers.
(C) Max sent the fax too late.
(D) Max Green and John Andersen already know each other.

Go on to the next page.

Questions 156 through 158 refer to the following notice.

NOTICE: To all patrons of the Blue Wave Fitness Center

The management would like members to note that the Blue Wave Fitness Center is not liable for any items left in the coin lockers. Should you lose anything from the locker, we regret that we will be unable to assist you in any way. Therefore, it is important that you make certain that your locker is kept locked while you are using our facilities. Also, for security reasons, we do not keep a record of members' locker combination codes, so it is vital that you remember the combination you choose.

156. Where would this notice be posted?

(A) In a changing room
(B) At a railway station
(C) In a restroom
(D) In an office

157. What do members need to open their lockers?

(A) A key
(B) Coins
(C) A series of numbers
(D) Nothing

158. Why do you think this notice was posted?

(A) The Blue Wave has suffered thefts recently.
(B) The Blue Wave changed its management.
(C) The Blue Wave has bought new lockers.
(D) The Blue Wave is looking for new members.

Justin,

Vera called to let you know that she has finished the files and has sent them by courier. You should be getting them this afternoon. She said to call her as soon as you get back from lunch. She wants to discuss some of the details about the plans before tomorrow's meeting. She said she is sorry for keeping them so long, but it has been really busy over at her branch, and she had to wait for Sam to get back from his business trip.

Susan

159. What was Justin doing when Vera called?

(A) Attending a meeting
(B) Talking on another line
(C) Having lunch
(D) Resting at home

160. What is Vera sending to Justin?

(A) A document
(B) Some files
(C) Lunch
(D) A phone call

161. Why didn't Vera send the files earlier?

(A) She forgot about them.
(B) She was away on a business trip.
(C) She didn't want to.
(D) She has been busy.

Go on to the next page.

To: satty98@hatmail.net
From: bcyo99@lions.co.sp
Subject: Recordings

Hi Samantha,

This is just a quick email to let you know that we have found enough voice actors to make the recording for the radio advertisement. The Heartful Acting Agency is providing us with three children who will work with the man and the woman you had already found. They are charging $50 an hour per child, so let's try to get it done as quickly as we can to keep costs down. I have given the agency the scripts.

See you at the studio.

Brian

162. Why did Brian send this email?

(A) To ask Samantha to find more actors
(B) To let Samantha know they have enough actors
(C) To tell Samantha about a meeting
(D) To complain to Samantha

163. How many voices will be used in the advertisement?

(A) Two
(B) Three
(C) Four
(D) Five

164. Why does Brian want to finish the recording quickly?

(A) He hates recording.
(B) He wants to save money.
(C) He has another appointment afterwards.
(D) He is impatient.

Saving Time When Computing

Here is the second installment in our monthly "Computing for Business Users" guides.

A common complaint among computer users is the amount of time they spend waiting for their laptop to start up and perform its tasks. Here are some handy tips on how to eliminate some of that waiting time.

- Don't shut your laptop all the way off between meetings; just put it in the low-battery consumption "Standby" mode. Shutting it down and waiting for it to reboot at the next meeting wastes valuable time. This way you are ready to start as soon as you arrive.
- Having too many programs in your computer's Start Up folder really slows things down. The solution? Eliminate all unnecessary programs.
- Stop too many programs from running at the same time when you start up the computer. Don't know how? It's easy if you follow these instructions: click the Start menu, choose Run, then type "msconfig" to launch the System Configuration Utility. Next, on the "General" tab, click "Selective Startup." Then go to the "Startup" tab and uncheck any startup items that aren't necessary.

These are small but simple changes that you can make for yourself to save precious time. Next issue we'll be looking at extending your battery life.

165. Who is this article intended for?

(A) Computer programmers
(B) Business people
(C) Program designers
(D) Professional computer game players

166. What does the article explain?

(A) How to start up your computer
(B) How to improve the speed of a computer
(C) How to change a battery
(D) Where to buy the best computer

167. How often are these computer articles published?

(A) Every day
(B) Every week
(C) Once a month
(D) Twice a year

168. What is the topic of the next article?

(A) Buying a new computer
(B) Making your battery last longer
(C) Computer accessories
(D) Security

Go on to the next page.

Wanted: Graduate Manufacturing Engineer

The candidate should be a recently qualified engineering graduate with experience working both as a member of a team, and alone unsupervised. The ideal candidate will have background studies in the field of manufacturing engineering. The candidate should be open-minded and capable of dealing with a challenging, high pressure environment with a view to continuous improvement and development of manufacturing techniques.

This is a full-time position. The candidate will be required to work 40 hours a week, Monday to Friday, but thanks to our flex-time system, the successful candidate will be able to choose his or her working hours, within reason. The position pays a starting salary of £20,000, with the possibility of quarterly bonuses, dependent upon performance. A pay raise will be offered after 6 months, again depending upon performance. Good prospects for promotion. 15 days paid vacation in the first year, rising in subsequent years. Sponsorship for part-time study is also a possibility after one year's employment. Benefits include subsidized health insurance, company pension, subsidized use of company sports center, and use of child day care center.

Send résumé and cover letter to:

Lionel Blair
Personnel Manager

Grant Manufacturing,
Springhurst Industrial Estate,
Springhurst
NN0 223

Application deadline: December 15th. Only short-listed candidates will be contacted. No phone inquiries, please. Candidates who were unsuccessful in our previous recruitment campaign are kindly asked NOT to reapply.

169. What is the purpose of this advertisement?
   (A) To recruit a new engineer
   (B) To advertise something for sale
   (C) To introduce manufacturing engineering
   (D) To promote Grant Manufacturing

170. How often could an employee expect to receive a bonus?
   (A) Once a year
   (B) Twice a year
   (C) Four times a year
   (D) Never

171. Which of the following benefits is NOT mentioned?
   (A) Health insurance
   (B) Pension
   (C) Child care
   (D) Subsidized transportation

172. Who should NOT apply for this job?
   (A) Engineering graduates
   (B) People who like a challenging environment
   (C) People who previously applied for a job at Grant Manufacturing
   (D) People interested in promotion in their job

Go on to the next page.

Patel Pottery
16 Whitford Drive
Scranton, OH 40985
January 5, 2006

Mrs. Ivy Richards
209 Singlewell Road
Rochester, MD 10337

Dear Mrs. Richards,

Thank you for your recent inquiry about the range of goods produced by Patel Pottery. It is my great pleasure to send you a copy of our latest catalog.

We are a small family-run business, and as such, do not produce large quantities of any of our items. Each item that appears in our catalog is limited to a production run of 10. This means that only ten of each item is ever produced.

On occasion, if a particular item produces a great demand, then we may recreate it, but we prefer to keep the individuality of our products and steer clear of mass production. This is because of our philosophy of craftsmanship. We feel that once our potters are asked to make things in large numbers, they risk losing the sense of craftsmanship and begin to feel like a mass production conveyor belt. Of course, this does mean that our prices are somewhat higher than in the average store, but I am sure you will agree that it is worth the cost to be able to own a more unique piece of pottery.

If you see anything in our catalog that catches your eye, or if you have a design of your own that you would like made, the best way to place an order is to call me at 088-799-8000. You can also check out our website at www.patelpot.co.uk.

I hope to hear from you soon.

Sincerely,

Ranjiv Patel,
Orders and Deliveries Manager

173. Why did Mrs. Richards write a letter?

   (A) To get information about Patel Pottery's products
   (B) To place an order
   (C) To make a complaint
   (D) To ask a favor

174. What does Ranjiv Patel say about the price of their goods?

   (A) They are cheap.
   (B) They are rather expensive.
   (C) He doesn't mention prices.
   (D) They are the cheapest in town.

175. What is Ranjiv Patel's responsibility?

   (A) Design
   (B) Answering complaints
   (C) Taking and dispatching orders
   (D) Advertising

176. How should Mrs. Richards place an order?

   (A) By email
   (B) By visiting the pottery
   (C) By letter
   (D) By phone

Go on to the next page.

To: All Kitchen staff
From: Food & Beverage Services
Re: Food hygiene
Date: September 12th

A few days ago, I was disturbed to learn that the front desk has been receiving complaints about the quality of food served by our kitchens. Last week, there were four complaints about hair being found in food. This week, there have been several complaints about soil and insects in the salad from lettuce which has been insufficiently washed. And the last straw, this morning one of our customers found a false nail in her scrambled eggs at breakfast.

I am not going to point fingers, but I would like to say that all of these complaints were made on Thursdays and Fridays. While this is not necessarily conclusive, it does rather suggest to me that the source of these problems is likely to be someone who works on these two days. This narrows it down to a small percentage of the kitchen staff.

However, as I said, I am not going to assign blame, but I do want to remind everyone that all kitchen staff must have their hair tied back and covered by a hat or hair net at all times. Fingernails must be kept short and free of any nail polish or nail extensions. As for the incident of insufficiently washed lettuce, there is no excuse for this, and I expect all staff to be most assiduous in checking that all food is prepared perfectly before it is allowed to leave the kitchen.

177. Why was this memo sent?

    (A) Because there have been several complaints from customers

    (B) Because customers have been praising the food

    (C) Because the kitchen will soon be closed for renovations

    (D) Because Food & Beverage Services sends a memo every month

178. Who might be at fault in this situation?

    (A) All the kitchen staff

    (B) Someone who works on Thursdays and Fridays

    (C) The chef

    (D) A waiter

179. Which of the following items was NOT found?

    (A) A false fingernail

    (B) A tooth

    (C) Dirt and insects

    (D) Hair

180. How will the guilty person be punished?

    (A) He or she will have to wear a hair net.

    (B) There is no mention of punishment in the memo.

    (C) He or she will be fired.

    (D) He or she will pay a fine.

Go on to the next page.

Questions 181 through 185 refer to the following agenda and minutes.

Agenda for the INSCAN 5ᵗʰ Annual Public Board Meeting
Meeting date and time: June 22, 2005 2:25 p.m.
Location: Room 43

- Presentation of minutes from the last meeting

Reports

- Report from the President and CEO
- Report from the Chair of the Systems Advisory Committee
- Finance Committee's report

New Business

- Budget changes
- Election of new Chair of Finance Committee

Announcements
Adjournment of the meeting

John,

Here is a copy of the minutes from the meeting on June 22ⁿᵈ. Take a look and let me know what you think before I make copies to send to everyone. I lost the notes which I made at the meeting, so tell me if you remember things being the way that I have described.

Minutes
The meeting opened with a reading of the minutes of the last meeting by secretary Jenny Schmidt. These were approved by Anthony Woodward, meeting chair, and seconded by Francisco Alton, CEO.

The President and CEO read a report of the company's developments over the past year. This was followed by a report from the Systems Advisory Committee. The committee was pleased to report that all new systems implemented since the previous meeting have been successfully adopted throughout the company in all branches nationwide. Chair of the committee, Tina Alvarez, noted that the Chain of Command system has been particularly effective in improving interdepartmental communications. This has lead to a reduction in errors in data-inputting and a reduction in the number of employees complaining that they have not been informed of changes. This report was followed by the Finance Committee report which was also read by Tina Alvarez. According to the report, profits are up 3% from last year.

Budget changes for the coming fiscal year were explained, and a full account of these will be produced by the Finance Committee in due course. Elections for a new Finance Committee chair were held, with Max Hampstead winning.

Finally, CEO Francisco Alton announced plans to move the company headquarters to a new location in 2007, and the meeting was adjourned.

Thanks for taking a look. Talk to you later.

Jenny

181. How often does INSCAN hold public board meetings?

    (A) Five times

    (B) Once a year

    (C) Every month

    (D) Twice a year

182. Who is Tina Alvarez?

    (A) The CEO of INSCAN

    (B) The meeting chair

    (C) Chair of the Systems Advisory Committee

    (D) Chair of the Finance Committee

183. What has been the result of the Chain of Command system?

    (A) Better communications and fewer errors

    (B) Nothing of great value

    (C) Less employees being fired

    (D) A new chair being elected for the Finance Committee

184. What can be inferred from the letter?

    (A) Neither John nor Jenny attended the meeting.

    (B) Jenny, but not John, attended the meeting.

    (C) John, but not Jenny, attended the meeting.

    (D) Both John and Jenny attended the meeting.

185. Why did Jenny send a copy of the minutes to John?

    (A) She is sending a copy to everyone.

    (B) She wants him to check the accuracy of the minutes.

    (C) He asked her to.

    (D) It is John's duty to file the minutes of every meeting.

Go on to the next page.

Questions 186 through 190 refer to the following advertisement and memo.

To: Marie Hampstead, Joan Green, and Mark Southford
From: Helen Sorrell
Re: Advertisement
Date: March 1ˢᵗ

I am sending you all the first draft of the new advertisement for the summer cruises promotion campaign that we will be running in major newspapers and magazines throughout April and May. Please check through the copy and give me your feedback, which I will send to the advertising team responsible for this particular campaign. When you read through the advertisement, there are several things that I would like you to consider. It would be most helpful if you could refer to all of these in your feedback comments:

• Use of images: How do you think our target clients will respond to these? Will they appeal to the 20-30 age group that we hope to attract?

• Proportion of text to images: Is the advert too text-heavy, or have we achieved a good balance of words to pictures?

• Text content: Is it easy for people to extract the information they need quickly? Is the vocabulary we have chosen appealing to this age group? Will they identify with the message, or do we need to use more colloquial expressions and slang? Or have we used too much slang, and will it seem that we are in fact aiming at a younger teenaged audience?

Let me have your thoughts by March 4ᵗʰ. I'll arrange a meeting as soon as I have read everyone's feedback. Many thanks.

Think a cruise is just for grandpa and grandma? Think again!
Cruizin Cruises now has cruises just for people like you.

No one is over 30, and there is no shuffleboard or bingo. You'll be parasailing, swimming with dolphins, and partying all night. We welcome both couples and single passengers —singles can sign up for our on-board speed dating service.

No boring museums and walking tours: enjoy all night beach raves in the party capital of the world, Ibiza, and dance to top international DJs.

Call 091-993-4453 for more information or check out our website at www.cruiznfun.com.

186. What is the purpose of this memo?

    (A) To advertise a cruise company
    (B) To elicit feedback on an advertisement
    (C) To give feedback on an advertisement
    (D) To advertise a job on a cruise ship

187. Who do Cruizin Criuses hope to attract?

    (A) Elderly people
    (B) Teenagers
    (C) People in their twenties
    (D) Young families

188. When will the campaign be run?

    (A) Next year
    (B) In the summer
    (C) In April and May
    (D) March 4th

189. What may happen if the company uses too much slang in the advertisement?

    (A) People might feel the company wants to attract only very young customers.
    (B) People will think the company has poor writing skills.
    (C) The text will be difficult to read.
    (D) No one will be interested in the advertisement.

190. Who among the following would be interested in this cruise?

    (A) Someone interested in museums and art galleries
    (B) Someone who enjoys nightclubs and parties
    (C) Someone who enjoys sightseeing tours
    (D) Someone who wants a quiet getaway

Go on to the next page.

2009 Bear Circle,
Daviston, KS 23334
May 5th

Dear Sirs,

I recently purchased a new car battery at the Daviston branch of Advance Autoparts. The mechanics installed this battery for me, and I drove home. Once I arrived home, I read the receipt which I had been given. I noticed that there seemed to be some additional charges. I was charged for the following:

1. 1 car battery
2. Battery installation
3. Cable corrosion check
4. Cable cleaning
5. Reconnection of cables
6. Disposal of old battery
7. Mechanic's service fee
8. Tax

I feel that it is rather excessive to charge a separate fee for items 2 and 5. Connecting the cables is merely part of the installation process. I also feel that it is inappropriate to have charged an additional mechanic's fee--surely I am already paying the mechanic in item 2 for the installation.

Finally, I would have appreciated knowing in advance that I would be charged for disposal of the old battery. Had I known this, I would have liked to have taken it for disposal myself, since the public garbage disposal site does NOT charge a fee.

Perhaps Advance Autoparts would like to consider giving customers a breakdown of costs before carrying out repairs. I, for one, would probably not have used your services had I known exactly what I would be charged for.

Yours faithfully,

Ted Varani

Advance Autoparts
Byron Way
Daviston
May 10th

Mr. Varani
2009 Bear Circle
Daviston, KS 23334

Dear Mr. Varani,

I am writing in response to your letter of May 5th. I am sorry to hear that you feel our mechanics overcharged you. In fact, these are standard charges at all branches of Advance Autoparts. I think that you will also find that other car parts merchants and mechanics have similar charges.

I am sorry not to be able to offer any assistance in this matter, but I trust that you have been satisfied with the quality of the battery you purchased, and I am confident you will be happy with the quality of our mechanic's work.

Sincerely,

Kevin Heath,
Chief Mechanic, Advance Autoparts

191. Why did Mr. Varani write to Advance Autoparts?
    (A) He wanted to thank them.
    (B) He believed they had charged too much.
    (C) He wanted to order a new battery.
    (D) He wanted to find out their store location.

192. What does Mr. Varani think Advance Autoparts should give customers?
    (A) A list of costs before doing repairs
    (B) A free battery
    (C) An itemized bill
    (D) Free car wash and waxing

193. What would Mr. Varani have liked to have done for himself?
    (A) Dispose of the old battery
    (B) Install the new battery
    (C) Reconnect the cables
    (D) Check the cables

194. What will Kevin Heath do in response to Mr. Varani's letter?
    (A) Send a refund
    (B) Offer a free oil change
    (C) Nothing
    (D) Ask the mechanic to apologize

195. How does Kevin Heath feel about the quality of his company's service?
    (A) It could be better.
    (B) It is very good.
    (C) He expresses no opinion.
    (D) He is reluctant to say.

Go on to the next page.

Dear Executives,

Please take a look at the following chart. Attached for your consideration is a brief analysis of these figures compiled from results of all our stores. Please feel free to send us your feedback and comments.

With regards,
Happy Homes Financial Supervisory Committee

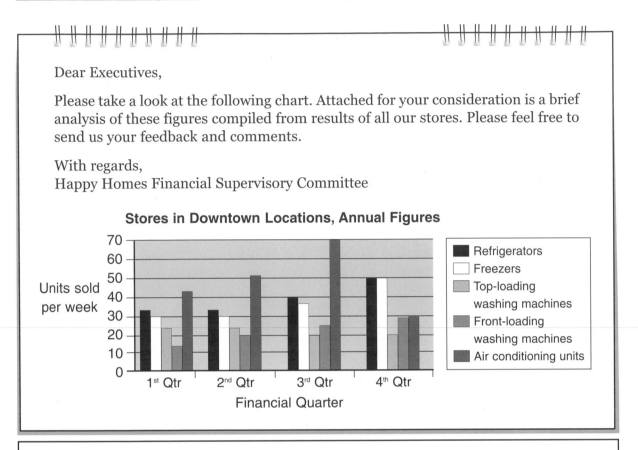

Stores in Downtown Locations, Annual Figures

The final figures for the financial year are out, and here is a brief analysis of what we have found. First, as you can see, we have charted the results for the following common household appliances: refrigerators, freezers, washing machines, and air conditioning units. As indicated in this chart, refrigerators remained a steady seller throughout the year. There was a rise in the fourth quarter of the year to an average weekly sale of 50 units. This can be explained by typical seasonal needs. With the advent of the Christmas and New Year period, many homeowners experience a lack of storage space for all the food they have in stock to serve guests and visiting relatives. We would like to suggest a bigger advertising campaign for the holiday season this coming year. Freezer sales show a similar rise in sales to refrigerators.

The third item in the chart is washing machines. Sales of washing machines were divided into two categories: top-loading and front-loading. This is where we noticed an interesting change. Traditionally, householders have favored larger top-loading machines. However, it can be seen on the chart above that the smaller front-loading machines are gaining in popularity, while sales of top-loaders are in fact decreasing. We are not exactly sure what has prompted this change, so we would like to propose a study to find out more about what people nowadays want out of a washing machine. Armed with the results of some market research, we will be better able to target customers with our advertising, and we will be able to put the right kind of machines in our stores.

Finally—air conditioning units. Sales have been steady with the usual seasonal fluctuations. Recent hot summers have tended to cause a larger number of sales in the third quarter, and this year was no exception. One change which is not visible on the chart: customers are tending to choose energy efficient models due to rising energy costs.

196. What information is contained in this chart and report?

(A) Sales results
(B) Profits
(C) Number of customer complaints
(D) Sales projections for the coming year

197. How many air conditioning units were sold in the first quarter?

(A) About 40
(B) About 50
(C) Less than 40
(D) More than 50

198. What causes an increase in refrigerator and freezer sales in the 4th quarter?

(A) Bargain sales are held in all locations.
(B) People give refrigerators as Christmas gifts.
(C) People need more space to store food for holiday guests.
(D) New models are produced for Christmas.

199. For which product is market research suggested?

(A) Refrigerators
(B) Freezers
(C) Air conditioners
(D) Washing machines

200. Which of the following is probably NOT sold at Happy Homes?

(A) Television sets
(B) Groceries
(C) Microwave ovens
(D) Toasters

Stop! This is the end of the test. If you finish before time is called, you may go back to Parts 5, 6, and 7 and check your work.

PRACTICE TEST

General Directions

This test is designed to measure your language ability.
The test is divided into two sections: Listening and Reading.

You must mark all of your answers on the separate answer sheet.
For each question, you should select the best answer from the answer choices given. Then, on your answer sheet, you should find the number of the question and fill in the space that corresponds to the letter of the answer that you have selected. If you decide to change an answer, completely erase your old answer and then mark your new answer.

LISTENING TEST

In the Listening test, you will be asked to demonstrate how well you understand spoken English. The entire Listening section of the test will last approximately 45 minutes. Directions are given for each of the four parts. There is a separate answer sheet for marking answers. Do not write your answers in the test book.

Part 1

Directions: In this part of the test, you will hear four statements about each picture in your textbook. After listening to all four statements, you must select the one statement that best describes what you see in the picture. Then find the number of that question on your answer sheet and mark your answer. The statements will be spoken only one time, and are not printed in your test book.

Sample Answer

Example

Now listen to the four statements.

Statement (B), "The woman is typing on a computer," best describes what you see in the picture. Therefore, you should choose answer (B).

1.

2.

Go on to the next page.

3.

4.

5.

6.

Go on to the next page.

7.

8.

9.

10.

Go on to the next page.

Part 2

Directions: In this section you will hear a question or statement followed by three responses. Select the best response to the question or statement and mark the letter (A), (B), or (C) on your answer sheet. Again, each response will be spoken only one time and will not be printed in your test book.

Example

You will hear: How are you today?

You will also hear: (A) I'm fine, thank you.
                     (B) It's cold, isn't it?
                     (C) Well, it's a difficult issue.

The best response to the question "How are you today?" is choice (A), "I'm fine, thank you." Therefore, you should choose answer (A).

11. Mark your answer on your answer sheet.

12. Mark your answer on your answer sheet.

13. Mark your answer on your answer sheet.

14. Mark your answer on your answer sheet.

15. Mark your answer on your answer sheet.

16. Mark your answer on your answer sheet.

17. Mark your answer on your answer sheet.

18. Mark your answer on your answer sheet.

19. Mark your answer on your answer sheet.

20. Mark your answer on your answer sheet.

21. Mark your answer on your answer sheet.

22. Mark your answer on your answer sheet.

23. Mark your answer on your answer sheet.

24. Mark your answer on your answer sheet.

25. Mark your answer on your answer sheet.

26. Mark your answer on your answer sheet.

27. Mark your answer on your answer sheet.

28. Mark your answer on your answer sheet.

29. Mark your answer on your answer sheet.

30. Mark your answer on your answer sheet.

31. Mark your answer on your answer sheet.

32. Mark your answer on your answer sheet.

33. Mark your answer on your answer sheet.

34. Mark your answer on your answer sheet.

35. Mark your answer on your answer sheet.

36. Mark your answer on your answer sheet.

37. Mark your answer on your answer sheet.

38. Mark your answer on your answer sheet.

39. Mark your answer on your answer sheet.

40. Mark your answer on your answer sheet.

Part 3

Directions: In this section of the test, you will hear a number of conversations between two people. You will be asked to answer three questions about what is said in each conversation. You must select the best response to each question and mark the letter (A), (B), (C), or (D) on your answer sheet. Each conversation will be spoken only one time and will not be printed in your test book.

41. Who has read the chairman's memo?

    (A) Ms. Reed
    (B) John
    (C) Turner
    (D) Westco

42. Why is the chairman's memo useful?

    (A) It can help with the Turner account.
    (B) It gives the vacation schedule.
    (C) It will help Ms. Reed negotiate prices.
    (D) It is well written.

43. Which account is Ms. Reed working on now?

    (A) The Turner account
    (B) The Reed account
    (C) The Westco account
    (D) John's account

44. What is needed in the man's office?

    (A) A fax machine and a copy machine
    (B) A tax machine and a copy machine
    (C) A tax machine and a coffee machine
    (D) A fax machine and a coffee machine

45. Where does she get her office equipment?

    (A) From the office supply store
    (B) From her friends
    (C) From an online retail supplier
    (D) From an online wholesale supplier

46. Orders over how much will be shipped free?

    (A) $10.00
    (B) $100.00
    (C) $1,000.00
    (D) $10,000.00

Go on to the next page.

47. What information does the man want?

(A) The airline schedule
(B) The work schedule
(C) The vacation schedule
(D) Peter's lunch schedule

48. Where is Peter?

(A) At lunch
(B) On vacation
(C) At the airport
(D) At his desk

49. Why does the man need the vacation schedule?

(A) To schedule his work
(B) To reserve a hotel
(C) To book an airline ticket
(D) To see Peter

50. How do you think Tom and Miranda know each other?

(A) Tom is her husband.
(B) Their companies sometimes work together.
(C) Tom often takes vacations.
(D) Tom is her manager.

51. What is Star Travel's commission on the Machu Pichu tour?

(A) Fourteen percent
(B) Forty percent
(C) Four percent
(D) Four hundred percent

52. What is Miranda's opinion of the Machu Picchu tour?

(A) It is too expensive.
(B) They should stay six more days.
(C) It may be dangerous.
(D) Many people will be interested in it.

53. What does Ann need for the meeting?

    (A) A projector, a table, and a dais

    (B) A table, a chair, and a key

    (C) A pen, some paper, and a notebook

    (D) His notes, his glasses, and some water

54. Why can't José bring the items?

    (A) He's been working too long.

    (B) He doesn't know where they are.

    (C) He is meeting with Mrs. Ames.

    (D) He doesn't have a key.

55. Who has a key to the equipment room?

    (A) Ted

    (B) José

    (C) Ann

    (D) No one

56. How will MegaStore contact him?

    (A) By waiting

    (B) By messenger

    (C) By phone

    (D) By mail

57. Why is his résumé impressive?

    (A) He has a lot of education.

    (B) He has a lot of work experience.

    (C) He has good references.

    (D) He included a good picture of himself.

58. Why does he think that he did not get the job?

    (A) He asked for too much money.

    (B) He forgot to send a résumé.

    (C) He is underqualified.

    (D) He is overqualified.

Go on to the next page.

59. When was the big meeting?

(A) This morning
(B) All day
(C) Yesterday
(D) Last week

60. Which department made a mistake?

(A) Product Development
(B) Finance
(C) Research
(D) Marketing

61. What will the man do?

(A) Make a new part
(B) Review the meeting minutes with the woman
(C) Talk to his boss
(D) Take new measurements

62. Which age group is targeted in the new ad campaign?

(A) Five to twenty-five years of age
(B) Fifteen to thirty years of age
(C) Fifty to twenty years of age
(D) Fifteen to twenty years of age

63. Who is advertising the product?

(A) An actor
(B) A singer
(C) An athlete
(D) A fashion model

64. Why isn't the ad successful?

(A) The product is too expensive.
(B) The actor's movie was not very good.
(C) The singer is no longer popular.
(D) The ad is offensive.

65. Why is the factory closing down?

   (A) The worker's wages are too high.
   (B) The cost of raw materials has gone up.
   (C) The product is not popular anymore.
   (D) The factory is moving.

66. When will the factory shut down?

   (A) It is operating in the red.
   (B) Next year
   (C) Next month
   (D) Next week

67. How many of the man's family members work at the factory?

   (A) Three
   (B) Two
   (C) All of them
   (D) None of them

---

68. How long had Louis worked for the company?

   (A) Less than one year
   (B) One year
   (C) More than one year
   (D) The reading does not say.

69. What is one thing that Louis and the boss disagreed on?

   (A) Where employees should take their breaks
   (B) How much employees should be paid
   (C) How employees should be motivated
   (D) When workers should be allowed to take vacations

70. Which answer best describes the relationship between Louis and the boss?

   (A) They are very good friends.
   (B) They are clearly angry with each other.
   (C) They never spoke to each other.
   (D) They kept a professional attitude even if they weren't friends.

Go on to the next page.

Part 4

Directions: In this section of the test, you will hear a number of short talks given by a single speaker. Again, you must answer three questions about what is said in each talk. Choose the most appropriate response to each question and mark the letter (A), (B), (C), or (D) on your answer sheet. Each talk will be spoken only one time and will not be printed in your test book.

71. What is Dr. Van Dyke probably doing right now?

    (A) Preparing to return to Australia
    (B) Setting up a conference room
    (C) Rehearsing for her afternoon lecture
    (D) Reviewing new marketing strategies

72. What is true of the Personnel Management Seminar?

    (A) The speaker announced its cancellation.
    (B) It has been moved to room 6A.
    (C) It is postponed until two o'clock.
    (D) The lecturer has a family emergency.

73. How many changes have been announced?

    (A) 2
    (B) 3
    (C) 4
    (D) 5

74. What might have prompted this announcement?

    (A) Some travelers' children have become lost.
    (B) An unattended bag was found.
    (C) Security officials have discovered weapons.
    (D) Airline counters have been shut down.

75. Who is asked to report to airline counters?

    (A) Travelers arriving at Terminal D
    (B) Those waiting to depart from Terminal D
    (C) People acting suspiciously
    (D) Those patrons who have only carry-on baggage

76. Who should passengers notify if they find unattended bags?

    (A) The police
    (B) Security or airline officials
    (C) The local media
    (D) Airport patrons

77. According to the message, what has Dr. Richards been treating Olga for?

(A) A hurt wrist
(B) A broken leg
(C) A painful shoulder
(D) A back problem

78. Why did Mr. Kerensky wait so long to cancel the appointment?

(A) He was not sure whether Olga needed to go.
(B) He wanted to thank Dr. Richards directly.
(C) He is not a patient man.
(D) He had simply forgotten about it.

79. Based on the message her father left, what is probably true of Olga?

(A) She is an elementary school student.
(B) Her injury is no longer bothering her.
(C) She wore her cast for only a short time.
(D) Her father worries about her health too much.

---

80. Who is Dr. Smiley?

(A) The lead chemist
(B) The director of research
(C) The head of personnel
(D) The orientation director

81. What is the focus of the talk?

(A) The morning's agenda
(B) An introduction to the company
(C) The three-day orientation
(D) Plans for after the tour

82. What is part of the planned tour?

(A) The personnel office
(B) The manufacturing site
(C) The employee lounge
(D) The company headquarters

Go on to the next page.

83. What is the final destination of the flight?

    (A) Auckland
    (B) Green Island
    (C) Bangkok
    (D) Wellington

84. What did the speaker tell the passengers to do?

    (A) Use their seat belts
    (B) Enjoy the weather
    (C) Prepare for take-off
    (D) Check their destinations

85. What is going to happen next?

    (A) The passengers will be served a meal.
    (B) The passengers will watch a safety video.
    (C) The flight attendants will serve drinks.
    (D) The captain will make a speech.

---

86. Who is this recording meant for?

    (A) Those shopping for copiers
    (B) People with questions about billing
    (C) Copier owners experiencing problems
    (D) Representatives of Nautilus Copier

87. Why is it suggested that the customer call back?

    (A) Nautilus Copier is currently closed.
    (B) The hold time is quite long.
    (C) He or she must first gather product information.
    (D) He or she must first contact another department.

88. What is located on the service agreement?

    (A) The warranty expiration date
    (B) The sales and service phone number
    (C) The purchase order number
    (D) The name of the company representative

89. According to the guide, how many waterfalls are higher than Tiger Falls?

(A) One
(B) Two
(C) Three
(D) Four

90. What experience does Mario think the tourists will find unforgettable?

(A) Walking through the dark caves
(B) Traveling to the top of the waterfalls
(C) Feeling the spray from the falls
(D) Viewing the falls from the underside

91. According to the talk, who will not receive raincoats?

(A) The tour guides themselves
(B) Persons who are very large
(C) Those riding in the elevators
(D) Tourists who have brought their own

---

92. What can be inferred from the broadcast?

(A) One plane collided with another.
(B) Condor Air is a major airline.
(C) The radio reported on the crash earlier.
(D) The helicopters will save some lives.

93. Who has survived the crash?

(A) No one
(B) One of the crew
(C) Several of the passengers
(D) It is not known.

94. Where did the incident occur?

(A) Over the mountains
(B) Over the sea
(C) In a field
(D) With the Coast Guard

Go on to the next page.

95. What kind of store is Antonia Francis probably calling?

    (A) A home supplies store

    (B) A supermarket

    (C) A bakery

    (D) A crafts store

96. Which of the following is NOT true?

    (A) Antonia has already paid for the cake.

    (B) The cake will be a chocolate sponge cake.

    (C) Antonia is organizing a birthday party.

    (D) The cake will be eaten by 50 people.

97. What can be inferred from the phone message?

    (A) Antonia has contacted the store before.

    (B) This is the first time Antonia has called the store.

    (C) The cake will be very popular.

    (D) It is a weekend.

---

98. What is the speaker trying to promote?

    (A) A new company

    (B) A new range of trash cans

    (C) A new trash collection system

    (D) His new invention

99. According to the speaker, how many different types of trash are there?

    (A) Two

    (B) Three

    (C) Four

    (D) Five

100. Which of the following items should be put in the blue box?

    (A) An empty cardboard box

    (B) An empty soda can

    (C) Tissue paper

    (D) Plastic bags

This is the end of the Listening test. Turn to Part 5 in your test book.

READING TEST

In the Reading test, you will be required to answer several types of reading comprehension questions based on a variety of texts. The Reading section of the test will last approximately 75 minutes. There are three parts, and directions are given for each part. You are encouraged to answer as many questions as possible within the time allowed.

You must mark your answers on the separate answer sheet. Do not write your answers in the test book.

Part 5

Directions: In each question, you will find a word or phrase missing. Four answer choices are given below each sentence. You must choose the best answer to complete the sentence. Then mark the letter (A), (B), (C), or (D) on your answer sheet.

101. Some customers have been ------- that the music in the dining area is too loud.

(A) praising
(B) satisfied
(C) complaining
(D) annoying

102. The boss was so angry at me that I was sure I ------- be fired.

(A) will
(B) would
(C) may
(D) might

103. Please do not assign Mrs. Beedle to a small office. She suffers from severe -------.

(A) hemophilia
(B) diabetes
(C) claustrophobia
(D) appendicitis

104. Intent on demonstrating its willingness to do what it takes to become a major force in the industry, Vetcom has taken very public measures to ------- top research and development experts away from other companies.

(A) deter
(B) beckon
(C) lure
(D) juggle

Go on to the next page.

105. ------- I am concerned, you may handle the situation in any way you deem fit.

(A) Inasmuch
(B) As to
(C) So much
(D) As far as

106. Women's groups continue to express outrage at what they perceive as ------- hiring practices in the industry.

(A) salutary
(B) inefficient
(C) contractual
(D) discriminatory

107. She said she ------- rather not meet with you face to face.

(A) had
(B) could
(C) did
(D) would

108. Labor leaders complain that even though the cost of living has nearly doubled in the past decade, workers' ------- have only increased by 14%.

(A) wages
(B) investments
(C) employees
(D) positions

109. At the upcoming board meeting, the chairwoman is expected to express ------- at the company's inability to improve its market share.

(A) offensiveness
(B) approbation
(C) assertiveness
(D) frustration

110. German trade representatives continue to pressure East Asian governments to reduce ------- on auto imports.

(A) tariffs
(B) finances
(C) cartels
(D) rebates

111. Richards was fired for abusing her ------- account privileges while on her last three business trips abroad.
   (A) deposit
   (B) expense
   (C) debt
   (D) savings

112. Employee benefits include paid holidays, medical and dental coverage, and a generous ------- plan.
   (A) pension
   (B) taxation
   (C) expansion
   (D) resignation

113. The store clerk notified security after ------- the shoplifter putting several pieces of merchandise into her purse.
   (A) revealing
   (B) observing
   (C) alerting
   (D) appealing

114. I will not be able to make the meeting, so my attorney will be negotiating on my -------.
   (A) behalf
   (B) beside
   (C) objective
   (D) objection

115. On your way out, please go to the front desk and ask the ------- to schedule your next appointment.
   (A) janitor
   (B) custodian
   (C) defendant
   (D) receptionist

116. You will be in my office with the finished report by five o'clock today, ------- I'll fire you! Got it?
   (A) nor then
   (B) in fact
   (C) or else
   (D) of course

Go on to the next page.

117. When I asked her whether the company had any plans for new investments, her ------- was simply a knowing smile.

(A) respond
(B) response
(C) responding
(D) responsive

118. Government tax officials regularly ------- the books of even medium-sized businesses to make sure they are paying their fair share to the national treasury.

(A) audit
(B) reflect
(C) measure
(D) maintain

119. Gretchen Curtis was ------- from assistant manager to manager because she has what it takes to lead this department.

(A) referred
(B) transferred
(C) promoted
(D) demoted

120. If only I ------- have to work tonight, I could ask her to the movie opening.

(A) did not
(B) might not
(C) shall not
(D) could not

121. I am not sure if this office is big enough for our needs; perhaps we need something a little more -------.

(A) cavernous
(B) enormous
(C) spacious
(D) precious

122. There is a saying, "The customer is always right," which simply means that a business should make customer ------- a top priority.

(A) satisfaction
(B) decisions
(C) loyalty
(D) comparison

123. Of course, I ------- if you sit down.

    (A) mind

    (B) don't mind

    (C) care

    (D) keep in mind

124. There are many factors to ------- before we make a final decision.

    (A) contribute

    (B) contract

    (C) confess

    (D) consider

125. I don't mind staying late every now and again, ------- don't expect me to be here every evening.

    (A) and

    (B) so

    (C) therefore

    (D) but

126. The board of directors voted ------- a 25% pay increase in their salaries.

    (A) itself

    (B) yourselves

    (C) themselves

    (D) herself

127. ------- was always one of my strong points during my M.B.A. course.

    (A) To advertise

    (B) Advertising

    (C) Advertisement

    (D) To advertising

128. My arm hurts. A bunch of us ------- blood today at work.

    (A) give

    (B) to give

    (C) gaved

    (D) gave

Go on to the next page.

129. She ------- always on time.

    (A) is

    (B) does be

    (C) are

    (D) be

130. She ------- spoken to me about your proposal.

    (A) did

    (B) have

    (C) is

    (D) has

131. There ------- no "I" in "Team."

    (A) be

    (B) isn't

    (C) ain't

    (D) is

132. You will find all the information you need ------- this computer disk.

    (A) on

    (B) in

    (C) at

    (D) by

133. The ------- is the first door on the right at the end of the hall.

    (A) label

    (B) labrador

    (C) labyrinth

    (D) lavatory

134. He tries hard, but I ------- don't think he is doing a good job.

    (A) very

    (B) really

    (C) almost

    (D) exceptionally

135. Please ------- when you are done with the computer.

    (A) lock off
    (B) lock on
    (C) log in
    (D) log out

136. We receive our ------- on the last Friday of every month.

    (A) paydays
    (B) paychecks
    (C) payment
    (D) parchment

137. I like this office ------- than my old one; it is much brighter.

    (A) better
    (B) more better
    (C) the better
    (D) the best

138. Tomorrow, I ------- going on a week-long business trip to the Maldives.

    (A) will
    (B) to
    (C) is
    (D) am

139. The receptionist keeps a(n) ------- in his ear to free both hands for typing.

    (A) telephone
    (B) receiver
    (C) earpiece
    (D) hairpiece

140. Honestly, I think my ------- is too low for all the work that I do.

    (A) celery
    (B) salary
    (C) solid
    (D) salve

Go on to the next page.

Part 6

Directions: Read the texts on the following pages. You will find a word or phrase missing in some of the sentences. Below each of the sentences, four answer choices are given. Select the most appropriate answer to complete the text. Then mark the letter (A), (B), (C), or (D) on your answer sheet.

Questions 141 through 144 refer to the following memo.

To: Graeme Lynch
From: Finance
Re: Taxes

It has been brought to our ------- that you have been charged incorrectly for taxes over the last five

      141. (A) notice
           (B) desk
           (C) attention
           (D) sign

months. We apologize sincerely because this is ------- to an error in our office. We were going

      142. (A) due
           (B) owed
           (C) indebted
           (D) resulted

through some personnel changes when you joined the company, and unfortunately some incorrect data was entered into our database. We have just realized that you have been charged for a higher tax bracket than you should have been. We are making ------- to rectify the situation immediately, and in

      143. (A) affords
           (B) results
           (C) designs
           (D) efforts

your next paycheck you will notice that less tax has been subtracted than in previous months. You can reclaim the previous extra deductions if you ------- for a rebate at the end of the financial year.

      144. (A) file
           (B) claim
           (C) hold
           (D) insist

Go on to the next page.

Questions 145 through 148 refer to the following letter.

Evergreen Garden Center
Slade Valley
Bradton
December 19th

Dear Mrs. Jane Goldby,

I am pleased to ------- you, on behalf of the Evergreen Garden Center, that this year, you are the

145. (A) oblige
(B) brief
(C) alert
(D) inform

lucky winner of our annual Christmas tree prize drawing. As you may recall from your last visit to our store, all customers ------- items during the month of December were automatically entered in our

146. (A) holding
(B) purchasing
(C) getting
(D) making

drawing. The winning tickets were drawn this morning, and you were the lucky first prize winner. A few other smaller prizes were also awarded. We would like to ------- you to a prize winners reception

147. (A) invite
(B) select
(C) invitation
(D) receive

at the Evergreen Garden Center on December 24th. Please let us know as soon as possible if you are unable to attend. We plan to present your prize on that -------.

148. (A) affair
(B) happening
(C) occasion
(D) event

Congratulations!

Sincerely,

Arthur Brown

Questions 149 through 152 refer to the following notice.

Today is the first year anniversary of the ------- of the Happy Valley Shopping Center. In celebration

149. (A) building
(B) start
(C) opening
(D) closure

of this fact, stores throughout the Happy Valley complex will be holding special events and big discount sales starting today and ------- for the next five days. Now is the time to check out all of your

150. (A) running
(B) completing
(C) organizing
(D) ran

favorite stores and maybe treat yourself to something nice. Shoes and boots will be half price on Monday. Coats and jackets will be marked ------- 25% on Tuesday. Home furnishings are priced

151. (A) up
(B) down
(C) in
(D) on

15% off on Wednesday, the bookstores are offering a 30% discount on novels on Thursday and on Friday, and the food court is ------- free meals to the first 200 customers! Don't miss out, and be sure

152. (A) outsourcing
(B) supplying
(C) serving
(D) creating

to tell your friends.

Go on to the next page.

Part 7

Directions: In this part of the test, you will read a selection of texts, such as magazine and newspaper articles, letters, and advertisements. Each text is followed by several questions. Choose the correct answer to each question and mark the letter (A), (B), (C), or (D) on your answer sheet.

From: Ken Nicholas. President, Nova Books
To: Heritage Credit Evaluations
Attention: Laura

Dear HCE,

This is to verify the employment of Dr. Lydia Rivers with Nova Books, a publishing firm headquartered in Kitchener, Ontario. Dr. Rivers is currently being compensated at the rate of $6,000 per month, but that sum is expected to increase as the pace of operations in the US picks up. Dr. Rivers has also been retained as a contract author/editor of educational materials to be published by Nova and the Nova children's line, Novino.

If you have any further questions regarding the employment status, creditworthiness, or character of Dr. Rivers, feel free to contact me.

Sincerely,

Ken Nicholas

153. Why might this fax have been sent?
    (A) To recommend Dr. Rivers for a job
    (B) To provide documentation to tax authorities
    (C) To support Lydia Rivers' application for a loan
    (D) To show that salaries are increasing quickly

154. What may happen as a result of this fax being sent?
    (A) Dr. Rivers should go to jail.
    (B) Dr. Rivers may be able to borrow money from a bank.
    (C) Dr. Rivers could lose her job.
    (D) Dr. Rivers will get a promotion.

155. What is Nova's children's book line called?
    (A) No kids
    (B) Novino
    (C) Nova youth
    (D) Young Novas

Go on to the next page.

The SunCool Hot Summer Wheels Contest

Purchase a 16- or 22-oz. bottle of any SunCool beverage, and you may spend a cool summer in the seat of a hot new Grand Z car, Apollo motorcycle, or Hi-Trekker mountain bike! Just look under the bottle cap and see if you are an instant winner.

(Rules and Details: Must be over 18 to play. One prize per contestant. Offer valid for US and Canadian residents only. Current employees of SunCool Corporation or members of their immediate families not eligible for prizes. Prizes must be redeemed by midnight, October 31, 2006. Odds of winning: car 1:400,000; motorcycle 1:45,000; bicycle 1:10,000.)

156. Based on the information in the ad, which of the following is most likely true?

    (A) This ad was published in a car magazine.
    (B) Most customers will win a prize.
    (C) SunCool is sold in more than one country.
    (D) There is only one flavor of SunCool.

157. Which of the following statements is clearly NOT true?

    (A) SunCool prints prize notices on the caps of its beverages.
    (B) One is more likely to win a car than a motorcycle.
    (C) No one may be awarded both a car and a motorcycle.
    (D) SunCool Cola is sold in more than one size bottle.

158. Who among the following cannot win an Apollo Motorcycle in this contest?

    (A) One who dislikes SunCool products
    (B) Someone born in November, 1995
    (C) A former SunCool executive
    (D) Someone not born in the US or Canada

Running Start Program:
Giving Kids a Running Start towards Education
Take part in the Price/Bellhouse Corporation Running Start Program

When: Saturday, July 15 @ 9:00 a.m.
Where: State University Athletic Complex

The Running Start Program is designed to supply children in need with a backpack, school supplies, and new clothing in order to prepare them for a successful school year. The money raised from the Price/Bellhouse Corporation's 5-kilometer run benefits the Running Start Program as well as other Combined Charities youth programs and services. Last year, with over 300 runners competing, more than $10,000 was raised—making all the kids served by Combined Charities the real winners!

159. What information is NOT contained in the promotion?

(A) The amount of money expected to be raised
(B) The names of the commercial sponsor
(C) The objectives of the Running Start Program
(D) The scheduled distance of the run

160. What best describes the event advertised?

(A) A state-sponsored inter-school competition
(B) An effort to improve student physical fitness
(C) A fund-raiser to help poor schoolchildren
(D) A race between employees of two companies

161. When is the event scheduled to be held?

(A) On a fall morning
(B) On a summer morning
(C) On a spring afternoon
(D) On a summer afternoon

Go on to the next page.

Questions 162 through 164 refer to the following instructions on an application form.

PHOTOS. You must submit 2 identical natural color photographs of yourself taken within 30 days of this application. The photos must have a white background, be unmounted, printed on thin paper, and not have been retouched. They should show a three-quarter frontal profile showing the right side of your face, with your right ear visible and with your head bare (unless you are wearing a headdress as required by a religious order of which you are a member). The photos should be no larger than 5cm x 5cm. With a pencil, print your name, application number, and the date taken on the back of each submitted photograph.

162. Which of the following is NOT a requirement for the two photographs?
(A) That they be taken the day before being submitted
(B) That they show the right side of the applicant's face
(C) That they be exactly the same
(D) That the date they were taken be indicated

163. What is the only requirement for which an exemption is stated in the instructions?
(A) The photos must be no larger than a certain size.
(B) The information on the reverse must be written in pencil.
(C) The head of the applicant must be shown bare.
(D) The background of the photo must be a specific color.

164. What should appear on the back of the photo?
(A) The application number
(B) The size of the photo
(C) The photographer's name
(D) The address

Questions 165 through 168 refer to the following product information.

Thank you for purchasing this CompuEd Product.

Our Product Development Philosophy

Since 1980, The CompuEd Company has consistently developed and marketed the most innovative and effective children's educational software available. Our award-winning products help develop your child's creative and cognitive abilities, while targeting important areas of school curriculum, such as reading, writing, social studies, and math.

Before hitting the market, every program from CompuEd is subject to extensive research and testing, with input from teachers, curriculum designers, education researchers, and—importantly—parents and children. Each product is designed not only to be educational, but also highly entertaining. In fact, our company's motto is, "For Learning to Get Done, Learning Must Be Fun."

CompuEd pioneered the use of Adaptive Learning Technology, whereby the software is designed and programmed to become more challenging as the skill level of the user increases. This means that it will be years before your child outgrows his or her CompuEd product!

Finally, CompuEd itself is continually learning from its customers. When we design new products or upgrades of existing products, we do so paying close attention to feedback from our consumers. So, if you have any comments or suggestions—positive or negative—please do not hesitate to pass them on to us. You can contact us via email at feedback@compued.com, or visit us on the web (www.home-compued.com) and fill out the customer comment form. The code for this product is math 42.

165. Where would this information most likely be found?
    (A) In a magazine advertisement
    (B) Included with purchased software
    (C) In a review of newly released programs
    (D) Attached to a letter from customer service

166. Which of the following would probably NOT be found on a CompuEd product's package?
    (A) "Learn geography with your favorite cartoon character!"
    (B) "Spend hours memorizing historical dates!"
    (C) "CompuEd: Over two decades of making learning fun."
    (D) "Prepare your child for the upcoming school year."

167. Among the following, who is NOT mentioned as being involved in the product development process?
    (A) Software engineers
    (B) Parents and their children
    (C) Researchers
    (D) Education professionals

168. According to the reading, which of the following is true?
    (A) CompuEd offers upgrades for all its older software.
    (B) CompuEd has been the most popular educational software since 1980.
    (C) CompuEd products have won awards in the past.
    (D) CompuEd's software is only for very young children.

Go on to the next page.

Questions 169 through 172 refer to the following job advertisement.

Part-time Help Wanted
School Bus Driver—Jones Transport Service

If you're a good driver who likes children, this is a great opportunity to plan ahead for a terrific part-time job during the school year!

Our small buses transport approximately 15 students to and from Steuben County schools within the greater Tri-State Area. At Jones Transport, you're guaranteed a minimum of 20 hours per week at $10.00 per hour after your training is complete. We even provide state minimum wage (currently $6.00) during training! We are now accepting applications for our summer training course. Only five positions will be filled, so hurry and act fast!

Parents, bring up to two preschoolers with you on the bus and save on day care expenses while you work!

Retirees, earn extra spending money and have the summer off to spend it! Live alone? Get out early each morning and enjoy contact with children and their parents.

All you need to bring to the job is the ability to relate well to school-aged children, an open, honest and enthusiastic attitude, and a level of comfort behind the wheel of a small school bus. We bring the rest! We are an equal opportunity employer and our training is covered by Veteran's Administration Benefits. Call us at 355-1128.

Please note that as per state law 45-119640a(g).i4 we cannot employ anyone who has been convicted of drunk driving or any felony. This law applies to convictions within the state as well as within other states. No exceptions will be made to this policy.

169. What is the hourly salary for people while training at Jones Transport?
    (A) It is $6.00 per hour.
    (B) It is $10.00 per hour.
    (C) People who are training do not get paid.
    (D) It depends on the number of students per bus.

170. Why should applications be submitted as soon as possible?
    (A) The summer training course has already started.
    (B) The school year will start by the end of the month.
    (C) Only a limited number of positions will be filled.
    (D) Jones Transport buses start running early.

171. Who is NOT specifically encouraged to apply for the job?
    (A) People who live alone
    (B) Residents of Steuben County
    (C) Retired people
    (D) Parents with young children

172. How many students usually take the bus each day?
    (A) Five
    (B) Fifteen
    (C) Fifty
    (D) Fifty-five

Go on to the next page.

MORGANTOWN—After 16 weeks of labor contract disputes, Costas Metals workers say they have had enough. At 10:30 this morning, hundreds of employees walked out of work and onto the picket line. Costas Metals employs more than 800 workers, and the union says about 90 percent of them are participating in the strike. They plan to continue to picket factory offices here in four hour shifts. The union representative claims workers have taken these measures as a last resort. "The membership had met and decided to wait for the company to put a decent offer on the table, and when it finally did late last night, it turned out to be wholly unacceptable. So, we voted to strike." The representative said that union members will strike as long as necessary, be it "one week or one hundred." Extra security has been ordered by the plant, and guards are blocking passage through the main entrance to the factory. Company officials have refused to comment on the situation. Local business leaders are concerned because any kind of prolonged dispute could have a negative effect on other sectors of the community as well. According to Hank Jarvis, owner of Jarvis Real Estate, "What happens to Costas Metals happens to our town." This attitude is shared by others as well. "Costas Metals is the backbone of our local economy. Everything from food to entertainment, to houses... it all connects to the metal plant," says one business owner who does not want to be identified. The whole town is hoping for a settlement soon.

173. What would be the best headline for this news report?

    (A) Costas Plant Orders Extra Security

    (B) Over 800 Workers Stage Walkout at Costas

    (C) Costas Metal Loses Money During Strike

    (D) Costas Workers Start Strike Today

174. What triggered the strike?

    (A) 16 weeks of continuous labor disputes

    (B) An offer by the company that the union found unacceptable

    (C) 90% of the workers picketing the factory offices

    (D) The company ordering extra security guards

175. How long do the workers intend to strike?

    (A) For four hours

    (B) A number of weeks

    (C) Indefinitely

    (D) Late into the night

176. If some of the plant workers were to lose their jobs, what might the effect on the community be?

    (A) No effect. Things would stay the same.

    (B) There would be more houses available for other people to live in.

    (C) The economy of the community would suffer.

    (D) The economy of the community would prosper.

Go on to the next page.

Attention All Food Mart Associates:

There are two matters that I would like to bring to your attention.

First, beginning tomorrow, April 5th, the city will be conducting repairs on the water lines under the north parking lot, and they expect to finish sometime around the 15th. While the north lot is closed, you may leave your vehicles in the main customer parking lot, but if you do, you must park as far away from the main entrance as possible. If an employee's vehicle is found parked near the store entrance, that employee will lose the right to park anywhere on store property. Remember, if you don't want to have to park on the street, please park your vehicles away from the store entrance. Your cooperation in this matter is greatly appreciated.

Second, there has been a problem with people going through the dumpster bins behind the store looking for food. We ask all employees to make sure that the dumpsters remain locked at all times, unless trash is being emptied into them. While the management understands and is sympathetic to the needs of the less fortunate who may be looking for food, the attorneys for Food Mart have warned us that for insurance reasons, the dumpsters must remain locked with both a padlock and a chain. Also, if you see anyone going through the dumpster bins, please report them to the management. Thank you again for your cooperation.

Kurt Bokonon
Assistant Manager

177. For whom is this message intended?

    (A) The assistant manager
    (B) Employees of Food Mart
    (C) City repair personnel
    (D) Food Mart customers

178. How long will the north parking lot be closed?

    (A) Around 10 days
    (B) For 15 days
    (C) From tomorrow until April 5th
    (D) While the customer lot is used

179. It can be inferred that employees usually park their vehicles in what location?

    (A) The north parking lot
    (B) On city streets
    (C) Away from the store
    (D) The main parking area

180. What is the store's problem related to the dumpsters?

    (A) The dumpsters are too small for all of the garbage.
    (B) People are taking things out of them.
    (C) An employee lost the key for the padlock on the dumpster.
    (D) Animals are getting into the dumpsters because they aren't locked.

Go on to the next page.

Questions 181 through 185 refer to the following faxes.

FAX: URGENT

To: Samantha Curnow, Leila Fashions
From: Annette Lyons, Head of Ladies Fashions, Alderson Department Store
Re: Order
Date: December 15th

Sam,

The clothes and shoes that you sent us in the last delivery have proved to be an amazing success. They are just flying off the racks. Therefore, I would like to place an order for the following items:
An additional 5 dresses in each of the sizes you delivered before (a total of 50 dresses);
7 skirts in sizes 6 through 12 (even sizes only, a total of 28 skirts);
4 blouses in sizes 6 through 18 (2 pink and 2 black, even sizes only, a total of 28 blouses); and if you have any of those silver and pearl earrings, send us as many as you can. We want to have the clothes ready to go on sale within the next couple of days. Can you get them to us by midday on the 17th?

Let me as soon as you can,

Thanks,

Annette

FAX

To: Annette Lyons, Alderson Department Store
From: Samantha Curnow, Leila Fashions
Re: Order
Date: December 15th

Dear Annette,

I'm sending this fax in reply to the fax you sent early this morning. I've spent the morning telephoning around our suppliers and factories, trying to gather all of the items you have requested. Unfortunately, this being the holiday season, the factory we use on a regular basis is already working at full capacity, trying to complete orders from other clients. I've tried to pull a few strings and get some favors done, but I'm not having a lot of luck. What I can do is send you everything that we currently have in stock immediately, and try to get the other stuff to you later, if at all. I doubt that we will be able to get the rest of your order made before Christmas, and I imagine that you won't want to be stocking these items once Christmas has passed and you start moving into the bargain sale season.
Let me know what you think.

Regards,

Samantha

181. Why were these two faxes sent?

    (A) To discuss an order of clothes
    (B) To cancel an order
    (C) To discuss Christmas plans
    (D) To discuss the bargain sale season

182. Why does Annette want more of the same items?

    (A) The shelves look empty.
    (B) There is a great demand for them.
    (C) She wants to buy some for herself.
    (D) She is flying to a meeting.

183. What is the problem at the factories?

    (A) They are closed for the holidays.
    (B) They are busy fulfilling other orders.
    (C) They are going out of business.
    (D) There is no problem.

184. What has Samantha been doing all morning?

    (A) Christmas shopping
    (B) Telephoning manufacturers and suppliers
    (C) Making clothes
    (D) Making deliveries

185. How likely is it that Samantha will be able to send everything that Annette wants?

    (A) There is a very high possibility.
    (B) She had already sent the items.
    (C) She gives no indication of this.
    (D) It is very doubtful.

Go on to the next page.

Questions 186 through 190 refer to the following complaint and response.

To: Customer Response (customer.care@hanley.co)
From: zelda22@hipmail.com
Subject: Faulty goods
Date: May 19, 2006

I found this address on the side of the packet of one of your products, so I hope this is the correct address for complaints. If not, would you please forward this to the correct address? I am emailing you because of a problem that I experienced with a Hanley Electronics product. I have been using Hanley products for many years, and this was the first time that I have had any trouble. I recently purchased the Hanley Magic Straight/Wave Hair tongs from the online shopping mall on your website.

I had seen them advertised on television and in various fashion magazines. The problem is that even after waiting the recommended 5 minutes, the tongs did not really seem to heat up. I waited a further 5 minutes, but they still didn't get any hotter. I tried using them to straighten my hair, but nothing happened, and it was a waste of time. I would, therefore, like to receive a refund. Could you tell me how I should go about this?
Thank you for your time.

Zelda Whitfield

To: zelda22@hipmail.com
From: Alison O'Brian (aobrian@hanley.co)
Subject: Re: Faulty goods
Date: May 20, 2006

Dear Ms. Whitfield,

Thank you for your email alerting us to the problem you have had with one of our products. I am sorry to hear that this has inconvenienced you. This is the first complaint of this kind regarding this particular product, and I can only imagine that a wire has become disconnected. We would be happy to refund your money in full, including postage and packing. To obtain a refund we ask you to send the product (in its original packaging if possible), together with your name and address and order reference number to the following address:
Returns
Hanley Electronics
Byways Industrial Estate
Sacramento, CA 90786

Again, I apologize for any inconvenience and hope you will continue to use our products.
Sincerely,

Alison O'Brian

186. Why did Zelda Whitfield send an email?

    (A) To place an order
    (B) To ask for her money back
    (C) To ask for an exchange
    (D) To demand an apology

187. Which of the following statements best describes Zelda Whitfield?

    (A) She is a new customer.
    (B) She doesn't often make electronics purchases.
    (C) She frequently makes complaints.
    (D) She is a loyal customer of Hanley Electronics.

188. How long did Zelda Whitfield wait for the tongs to heat up?

    (A) 5 minutes
    (B) A total of 10 minutes
    (C) 15 minutes
    (D) Many years

189. How many other complaints has the company received?

    (A) None for this particular product
    (B) A dozen
    (C) Several
    (D) Hundreds

190. What information should Zelda Whitfield send?

    (A) Phone number
    (B) Credit card number
    (C) Name, address, and reference number
    (D) Name and email address

Go on to the next page.

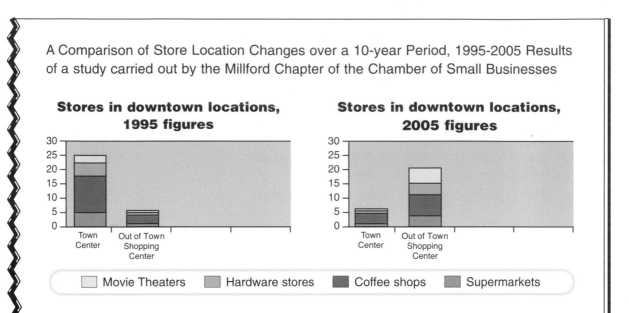

A Comparison of Store Location Changes over a 10-year Period, 1995-2005 Results of a study carried out by the Millford Chapter of the Chamber of Small Businesses

Stores in downtown locations, 1995 figures

Stores in downtown locations, 2005 figures

☐ Movie Theaters ☐ Hardware stores ■ Coffee shops ■ Supermarkets

Chamber of Small Businesses
Millford Chapter
304 High Street
Millford
January 22nd

Mayor Wesley
City Hall
Millford

Dear Mr. Mayor

As the chairperson of the Millford chapter of the Chamber of Small Businesses, I am sending you the attached charts for your consideration.

The Chamber of Small Businesses is concerned with conserving downtown shopping areas as we feel these provide a vital life source to any town. Unfortunately, these days, far too many of our town centers are being allowed to die. You may feel that this is rather over-exaggerated, but I'd like you to consider this: in a town center with empty boarded-up stores, crime rates rise. With no people around, these empty buildings become a den for drug addicts and dealers. Violent crime increases in empty streets. Young people cannot feel a sense of pride in their hometown if there is nothing left to feel proud of. Furthermore, in the past, young people grew up surrounded by small locally-owned businesses. This gave them something to aspire to. They saw other people from backgrounds like their own, who had become successful. Now, all they see is failure and big out-of-town stores owned by outsiders.

The Chamber of Small Businesses has long been concerned by the loss of small locally-owned businesses in Millford. If you look at the attached charts, I think you'll understand why. As you can see, even just ten years ago we had a reasonable range of stores, with a choice of proprietors so that we all had our favorite hardware store, or our favorite supermarket, often within walking distance of our homes. Over the past ten years, most of those stores have gone out of business unable to cope with the competition from the larger retailers set up in the new commercial estates on the outskirts of the town.

We urge you to promote businesses to set up in downtown locations and to set more restrictions on the construction of commercial areas on the outskirts of Millford. Let's bring life back to Millford.

Thank you for your time.

Sincerely,

Maurice Stiles,
Chamber of Small Businesses

191. What is the purpose of this letter?

    (A) To ask for permission to open a new business

    (B) To complain about crime in Millford

    (C) To express concern about the downtown retail area

    (D) To thank the mayor for his endeavors to bring new businesses to Millford

192. Who is Maurice Stiles?

    (A) Mayor of Millford

    (B) A member of an organization concerned with protecting small businesses

    (C) A crime prevention vigilante

    (D) The owner of a hardware store in downtown Millford

193. Which statement best describes the situation in Millford?

    (A) Between 1995 and 2005, all downtown coffee shops went out of business.

    (B) Between 1995 and 2005, all businesses relocated to out of town shopping centers.

    (C) In 2005, only coffee shops seem to have remained successful downtown.

    (D) In 2005, hardware stores are the most successful downtown retailer.

194. According to the letter, what is the result of a loss of small businesses downtown?

    (A) Rising prices

    (B) Higher unemployment

    (C) Less tourists

    (D) Rising crime

195. What does the Chamber of Small Businesses want the mayor to do?

    (A) Stimulate the downtown area and limit out-of-town retail areas

    (B) Open his own business

    (C) Resign from his position

    (D) Visit the Chamber of Small Businesses to give a speech

Go on to the next page.

Wanted: Graduate Manufacturing Engineer

Position offered: Cook
Employer: The Riverside Bar

We are a riverside attraction located on the south bank of the river Thames in London. Our bar carries a small lunch and dinner menu. We also provide corporate buffet food. We have a small, basic kitchen equipped with new appliances (all less than 6 months old). We are looking for one person who will work alone to carry out the duties described below:

Cooking
Receiving and putting away deliveries
Making orders when required
Cleaning the kitchen area
Serving in the bar if necessary

The ideal candidate will have at least 2 years experience working in the catering industry. We need a self-starter able to work without supervision, but also willing to help out at busy times. As a small business it is essential that all our employees are able to work as a team.

This is a permanent position paying £9 an hour.
Applications must be received by June 3rd.
Click here to apply:

Apply Now

From: ivynewn@lyan.net
Subject: Job Application
Date: May 30th

It is with great interest that I read the advertisement for a cook placed on the Jobs for All website. I am attaching my résumé for your consideration. I have over 7 years' experience in the catering industry. I started out as a bartender in the pub run by my family, then attended the local community college in order to qualify as a cook. I have been working as a cook at the Wayside Inn for the last 2 years. I am enjoying my current position, but would like to move to a job which allows me to have a little more responsibility. I am able to provide references from all my previous employers, should you need them.

I look forward to hearing from you.

Sincerely,

Ivor Newnham

196. What is the purpose of the advertisement?

    (A) To recruit a cook

    (B) To promote a new bar

    (C) To promote sightseeing in London

    (D) To give directions how to find a bar

197. Which is true of the Riverside Bar?

    (A) It does not serve food, only drinks.

    (B) It is a restaurant inside a large London hotel.

    (C) It has relatively new equipment in the kitchen.

    (D) It is not really located near a river; it is in downtown London.

198. Why does Ivor Newnham want to change jobs?

    (A) He hates his current job.

    (B) He wants more money.

    (C) He wants more responsibility.

    (D) He wants to move to London.

199. What kind of person is the Riverside Inn looking for?

    (A) A young person looking for their first catering job

    (B) An independent, cooperative person with a few years' experience

    (C) Someone who wants to work around a lot of other people

    (D) Anyone who can cook

200. Which of the following duties is NOT mentioned in the advertisement?

    (A) Cooking

    (B) Making deliveries

    (C) Cleaning

    (D) Making orders

Stop! This is the end of the test. If you finish before time is called, you may go back to Parts 5, 6, and 7, and check your work.

TRANSCRIPTS

& ANSWER KEY

PART 1. Picture Description

1. (A) The man is watching television.
   (B) The man is doing exercises.
   (C) The man is reading the newspaper.
   (D) The man is looking at papers.

2. (A) The office workers are watching a whiteboard.
   (B) The office workers are looking at a whiteboard.
   (C) The people are taking a whiteboard.
   (D) The people are cleaning a whiteboard.

3. (A) The man is a cooker.
   (B) It is being cooked.
   (C) The chef is working.
   (D) The chief is working.

4. (A) There is no one in the store.
   (B) The store is crowded.
   (C) It is bargain sale time.
   (D) She is trying on a coat.

5. (A) The man is taking the phone.
   (B) The man is talking to a woman.
   (C) The man is taking a phone call.
   (D) The man is hanging up.

6. (A) The bicycle is lying on the stairs.
   (B) The bicycle is next to a car.
   (C) The bicycle is hanging from the tree.
   (D) The bicycle is between a tree and the stairs.

7. (A) The desk is clean.
   (B) The desk is a little untidy.
   (C) There is nothing on the desk.
   (D) The man is writing at the desk.

8. (A) The man is working in his office.
   (B) The man is walking down the escalator.
   (C) The man is getting on an airplane.
   (D) The man is waiting for a bus.

9. (A) The man is climbing the ladder.
   (B) The ladder is up against a window.
   (C) The ladder is leaning against the wall.
   (D) The ladder is broken.

10. (A) The house is being knocked down.
    (B) A house is being built.
    (C) The man is fishing in front of his house.
    (D) The man is eating lunch.

PART 2. Questions and Responses

11. Don't you have Saturdays off?
    (A) The weekend is coming soon.
    (B) We'll meet after that, then.
    (C) Usually, but not this week.

12. I'm having trouble concentrating on this.
    (A) Well, why don't we take a short break then?
    (B) You have to concentrate.
    (C) It's an important issue these days.

13. When is the New Jersey train supposed to arrive?
    (A) I'm not sure, I'll check.
    (B) Your ticket is not valid today.
    (C) It comes directly from Boston.

14. How do you plan to get that document there by Thursday?
    (A) I expect it to be.
    (B) By express mail.
    (C) Next Wednesday.

15. Could you look this over for me?
    (A) No, it can't be predicted.
    (B) Sure, but don't count on it.
    (C) Sure, I'll be there in just a second.

16. What do you think of the new vacation policy?
    (A) Yes, I certainly have.
    (B) I think it's a little unfair.
    (C) Not right at this moment.

17. Isn't that a terrific idea?
    (A) Yes, it's a terrible one.
    (B) Yes, absolutely brilliant.
    (C) No, I haven't any yet.

18. Are you going to Chicago by bus or train?
    (A) Neither, I'm flying there.
    (B) My brother drove me.
    (C) Yes, by bus.

19. Where is Jim McTaggart's office?
    (A) Yes, it's here.
    (B) Oh, I'm sorry.
    (C) It's on the fifth floor.

20. I'm sorry I had to put you on hold.
    (A) Here, give it to me.
    (B) I don't mind a little wait.
    (C) I can't accept your offer.

21. Whom do you think we should give the job to?
    (A) I'd say the first woman we interviewed.
    (B) I think that no one will regret it.
    (C) The application deadline was last week.

22. Do you have a personal assistant?
    (A) So far, so good.
    (B) No, I handle everything myself.
    (C) Yes, Nadia is leaving soon.

23. Why are you postponing the launch?
    (A) By at least two or three days.
    (B) Not everyone has time for lunch tomorrow.
    (C) Because we were instructed to.

24. When does your training begin?
    (A) It's over at twelve.
    (B) At the end of August.
    (C) Don't miss the start.

25. Where can I catch a taxi around here?
    (A) There's a taxi stand around the corner.
    (B) You can sit down if you want.
    (C) Yes, right around the corner.

26. Why did you take those files out of the office?
    (A) I wanted to read them over dinner.
    (B) That's a serious issue, you know.
    (C) Of course, but not for very long.

27. Do you want to look at the figures today or tomorrow?
    (A) I'm exhausted. Let's wait.
    (B) No, I'm not very hungry right now.
    (C) Yes, I want to look at them.

28. It looks like it might rain, doesn't it?
    (A) Put your heavy coat on.
    (B) I think it's already started.
    (C) Tell me whether or not to.

29. Are those service manuals available yet?
    (A) They don't serve that here.
    (B) Yes, if you don't mind.
    (C) No, but they will be soon.

30. You'll make it to Friday's training session, won't you?
    (A) It's hard for me to admit it.
    (B) I made it with my own two hands.
    (C) Yes, unless something urgent comes up.

31. Would you spell your last name for me, please?
    (A) Sure, it's C-R-U-Z.
    (B) It is a different pronunciation.
    (C) Last name, first name, middle initial.

32. Could you arrange a taxi for me this afternoon?
    (A) Sure, what time do you need it?
    (B) I borrowed it again last week.
    (C) This afternoon is not good for me.

33. Have you ever considered investing in the stock market?
    (A) Yes, I need to pick up some milk.
    (B) No, I prefer safer investments.
    (C) No, I wasn't able to then.

34. What are your summer hours?
    (A) August is the hottest month.
    (B) It stays light till late in the evening.
    (C) Store hours are the same all year.

35. Should we discount the prices or give away a free gift?
    (A) Personally, I like a good bargain sale.
    (B) It's a free gift.
    (C) I don't have a lot of time today.

36. When is the best time to call your office?
    (A) My phone number is 987-998.
    (B) Any time after 10:00 should be OK.
    (C) I don't have a receptionist.

37. Why hasn't Miguel arrived yet?
    (A) He called to say he's taking his son to the doctor.
    (B) He's not here yet.
    (C) Miguel is going to chair the meeting this afternoon.

38. How can I open the copier to remove jammed paper?
    (A) The jam will make it very sticky.
    (B) Oh, no. I've lost my papers.
    (C) Just pull the green lever on the side.

39. Would you recommend Jackson or Blake to print the new cards?
    (A) I don't particularly like the new design.
    (B) Jackson and Blake both received cards.
    (C) They're both good, but Blake is slightly cheaper.

40. When will you be ready to review the résumés with me?
    (A) How does 3 o'clock sound?
    (B) I haven't told them yet.
    (C) Well, that's just your opinion.

PART 3. Short Conversations

Questions 41 through 43 refer to the following conversation.

(M) Finally! I've been waiting for this shipment of fabric for nearly a month. I was beginning to think it would never arrive. Now I can get on with the dresses I'm making for Jayford's Department Store.

(W) That's a relief. The store has been calling every day about those dresses. What took it so long to get here?

(M) I don't know. Maybe it took a while to clear customs.

(W) No, look. They got the address wrong. No wonder it took so long.

Questions 44 through 46 refer to the following conversation.

(W) Hey Dean. You've been working on that same machine for a week! Do you think you can fix it? Maybe we should just replace it?

(M) I'm not ready to give up yet, but this is the most complicated repair job I've ever had to do. I'm having trouble reconnecting some of the wires. But I think I'll get it done before the end of the day.

(W) Well, I'm glad I just use computers and don't have to fix them.

Questions 47 through 49 refer to the following conversation.

(W) Oh, no. I don't have much cash on me. I thought I had more than this. Would you take a check instead?

(M) Yes, certainly. We accept personal checks provided they are accompanied with two forms of ID, including a driver's license. So as long as you have ID, I can take a check.

(W) Well, I don't drive, so I can't show you a driver's license. Would my passport work instead?

(M) That would do just fine.

Questions 50 through 52 refer to the following conversation.

(W) I noticed on the time sheet that you are coming in tomorrow. But it's a national holiday. Why are you coming in to work?

(M) Well, I don't really want to, but I'd like to get some cleaning and reorganizing done. I seem to have let things really pile up lately. I need to get on top of things.

(W) That's very admirable. I should come in, too. I've got a huge backlog of orders to work on, but I'm going to enjoy having the day off.

Questions 53 through 55 refer to the following conversation.

(M) I can't believe I overslept. It looks as though I'm going to be late for work again. I'm going to get into so much trouble. It's the third time this month.

(W) It's only 8:30. You can make it if you hurry.

(M) No way, I don't think I can get there in half an hour in rush hour traffic. My boss is going to kill me.

(W) Don't worry, I'm sure you'll get there in time.

Questions 56 through 58 refer to the following conversation.

(M) Excuse me, but is there a phone here I could use? I really need to make a phone call, but the battery on my cell phone is dead.

(W) Um, well, there's a payphone, but that's been out of order for the past couple of days. Try the shop next door. I'm sure they have a payphone.

(M) I did, but theirs is broken, too. Could I possibly borrow your cell phone?

(W) I'm sorry, but I never lend it to customers.

Questions 59 through 61 refer to the following conversation.

(M) I hope you don't mind me asking, but I know that you live near me, and I was wondering how you get to and from work.

(W) I take the bus on Mondays and Tuesdays, but my brother drives me the rest of the week.

(M) I see. I was wondering why I never see you on the subway.

(W) Well, the bus is a little cheaper than the subway, and my brother works a couple of blocks from here.

Questions 62 through 64 refer to the following conversation.

(M) You've been slaving away for hours. You didn't take a lunch break, did you? John and I are going for coffee, and I wondered if you'd care to join us?

(W) I'd like to, but I'm expecting an important phone call. I've been waiting all day, and I don't dare leave my desk in case I miss it.

(M) In that case, would you like us to bring something back for you?

(W) Well, if you don't mind, I'd love a large coffee and a blueberry muffin.

Questions 65 through 67 refer to the following conversation.

(W) Have you seen the proposed designs for the Tanaka Corporation headquarters in Singapore? I think it is going to look great. Amy and Hank have done a really good job.

(M) Yeah, but it looks as though they will have to make a few structural changes. The chief engineer found a few flaws.

(W) Oh, I hope they won't have to change the shape of the building too much. I really like the way it looks like a ship.

(M) Well, it is certainly appropriate for a shipping company.

Questions 68 through 70 refer to the following conversation.

(M) Is it true what I've heard about the personnel department? I can't believe it.

(W) Well, what have you heard? You know I'm always the last to hear the latest gossip.

(M) I heard that the manager of the personnel department has been fired, and they are going to reassign all the other personnel department employees to other departments.

(W) From what I've heard, he's leaving because he was headhunted by another company, and I think you spend too much time listening to gossip around the water cooler.

PART 4. Short Talks

Questions 71 through 73 refer to the following announcement.

(M) I hope you've all enjoyed tonight's dinner. It is now time to welcome this evening's guest speaker, Carol Draper. Ms. Draper is the editor-in-chief of *Investor's Weekly* magazine. She took over the position of editor just over 2 years ago, and in that short time, the magazine has become one of the most influential publications in finance. Ms. Draper is also a well-respected, best-selling author in the field of investment. She will speak tonight on long-term trends in interest rates, a subject she dealt with at length in her last book, *Money Moves*. Ms. Draper has also agreed to take questions from the floor after her talk. Let's have a big hand for Carol Draper.

Questions 74 through 76 refer to the following telephone message.

(W) You have reached the airport ticket counter of Eagle Rent-a-Car. Thank you for calling. We regret to inform you that we are currently closed. Operating hours at this location are from 7:00 a.m. to 9:00 p.m., Monday through Friday, and 8:00 a.m. to 8:00 p.m. on weekends. If you need rate information or would like to make a rental reservation at this time, please call our nationwide toll-free number, which is available 24 hours a day, or visit us on the Web at www.eaglerents.com. We look forward to serving you.

Questions 77 through 79 refer to the following announcement.

(M) Troy County Library patrons, may I have your attention, please. This is a public safety announcement. Due to an emergency maintenance situation, the children's section on the ground floor is being closed at this time. This section of the library has suffered a burst pipe. If you have children there, please escort them from the area. All other sections of the library will remain open today until our normal closing time of 9:00 p.m. In as much as we cannot predict the maintenance situation tomorrow, those planning to bring children to the library are advised to call before coming in. We apologize for the inconvenience and hope to have things back to normal as soon as possible.

Questions 80 through 82 refer to the following announcement.

(W) Attention Flo-Mart customers: If you want a great deal on batteries, just follow the flashing yellow light to our electronics department. Right now, as long as the yellow light is flashing, you can get 25-40% off name brand batteries in all sizes. Need batteries for your smoke detector, flashlight, or children's toys? How about the TV remote control? Get to the electronics department and pick them up at great savings. Hurry now and get those batteries you keep meaning to buy, or buy some to keep in stock. Remember, the discount is only good while the Flo-Mart yellow light is flashing. After that, it's back to our normal everyday low prices. You don't want to be the only one in town paying full price!

Questions 83 through 85 refer to the following weather report.

(M) You're listening to Newton Radio. Well, now it's fifteen past the hour, and time once again to move to the Climate Network's hourly nationwide weather update. Our top story today: there is still a tornado warning in effect in the South, where twisters earlier today killed four people and left dozens injured. The tornadoes destroyed dozens of buildings and have left hundreds homeless. Emergency workers are in the area tending to the injured and trying to find shelter for them before nightfall. Bad weather remains elsewhere in the country, also, as heavy rain continues to soak the western mountains. Some of our affiliated stations there are reporting up to five inches in the last 12 hours. Needless to say, many roads and highways are closed throughout the region.

Questions 86 through 88 refer to the following message.

(W) Congratulations, Paula Chen, you have been selected as a finalist in the $10,000 CNTA Radio Summer Bucks Contest. I hope you are listening, but as a big Jim and Tammy fan, I'm sure you are. To confirm your entry, all you have to do is call our station anytime tomorrow during the Jim and Tammy Morning Show, and you will be among the five finalists for the grand prize of $10,000. If we don't hear from you before the end of the show though, you'll be out of luck and out of the running for the money. Once again, make sure to call CNTA Radio during tomorrow's Jim and Tammy Morning Show. Good luck, and remember to keep your dial set to CNTA — Houston's favorite country music station!

Questions 89 through 91 refer to the following news report.

(M) Customs officials announced today that several employees of an unnamed country's United Nations delegation are being held at New York's John F Kennedy Airport on charges of attempted importation of narcotics. The officials have stated that none of the five suspects was carrying a diplomatic passport. As a result, the five are not immune from prosecution under US drug laws. Confidential sources have told this reporter that the suspects are all from the Republic of San Lorenzo, and that they were trying to smuggle heroin into the country. While this information is as yet unconfirmed, according to airport customs officials, there has been a rise in illegal drugs smuggled from San Lorenzo in recent months. As part of the government's new tougher guidelines on drug smuggling, the suspects face a minimum of 25 years' imprisonment, if convicted.

Questions 92 through 94 refer to the following announcement.

(W) Attention, all employees. There is a blue pickup truck in back of the plant that is blocking loading ramp number six. Would the owner of this vehicle, license plate number CA990, kindly remove it? It must be moved immediately as it is blocking deliveries. Once again, a blue pickup truck, with the license plate CA990 is blocking a loading ramp, and it must be moved right away. If the vehicle is not moved in the next ten minutes, it will be towed away at the owner's expense. We ask you to please note that parking is available across the street in the pay-and-display parking lot. We urge you to use this parking lot during the plant's operational hours for all vehicles not involved in deliveries.

Questions 95 through 97 refer to the following announcement.

(M) Ladies and gentlemen, we would like to welcome you aboard the Capital Express, the only non-stop service to Washington. If this is your first trip on the Express, you are about to experience rail service like no other in the country. The Capital Express is the fastest passenger train operating in North America, reaching speeds of up to 105 miles per hour. (For our international passengers, that's 175 kilometers per hour.) Today's trip to Washington will take just over three hours, compared to the nearly six hours that it takes on a conventional train. To make your journey even more pleasant, we will be offering a refreshment service as soon as the train departs. Choose from a selection of teas and coffees, cold drinks, and tasty snacks. Enjoy your ride.

Questions 98 through 100 refer to the following telephone message.

(W) Larry, it's mom. I forgot to tell you this morning, but I have something going on after work today and won't be home until eight, so I won't be able to get dinner ready for you tonight. Go ahead and fix yourself some dinner whenever you're hungry. There's a pizza in the freezer, so you can help yourself to that if you want it. Have a salad or some other vegetables with it, though, OK? And you can have some ice cream, too, if you'd like, but don't take too much. Oh, and I don't mind if you watch TV, but don't invite anyone over and be sure to get your homework done before I get home. I don't want you staying up late because you didn't do it earlier.

PRACTICE TEST 2

PART 1. Picture Description

1. (A) The woman is learning about the pillar.
   (B) The woman is leaning on the pillar.
   (C) The woman is sitting against the pillar.
   (D) The woman is leaning on the sign.

2. (A) The filing cabinet is empty.
   (B) The filing cabinet is open.
   (C) There is nothing in the drawer.
   (D) The filing cabinet is closed.

3. (A) The woman is walking to her office.
   (B) The woman is on her lunch break.
   (C) The woman is carrying heavy boxes.
   (D) The woman is working in her office.

4. (A) The restaurant is very popular.
   (B) The restaurant is close to the bar.
   (C) The restaurant is closed.
   (D) The restaurant has many customers.

5. (A) The man and woman are talking.
   (B) The man is taking a picture.
   (C) The woman is taking a picture.
   (D) The man is taking the woman's wallet.

6. (A) The man and woman are being served by
       the waitress.
   (B) The waitress is being ordered by the woman.
   (C) The man and woman are taking a vacation.
   (D) The waitress is drinking tea.

7. (A) People are sitting opposite the shopping mall.
   (B) The man is beside the shopping mall.
   (C) There are cars parked in front of the shopping
       mall.
   (D) There is a line of people across from the
       shopping mall.

8. (A) The people are pointing at the form.
   (B) The man is filing some documents.
   (C) The woman is filling out a form.
   (D) The man has filled out the forms.

9. (A) The man is standing in a supermarket.
   (B) The man is waiting for a bus.
   (C) The man is standing in a hardware store.
   (D) The man is serving customers.

10. (A) There is a large vase on the reception desk.
    (B) There is a large vase on the table in the lobby.
    (C) The vase is next to the man.
    (D) A woman is arranging flowers.

PART 2. Questions and Responses

11. Excuse me, where is the fax machine?
    (A) It's not working properly.
    (B) Down the hall and to the right.
    (C) No problem.

12. Why doesn't she ever come to the safety
    meetings?
    (A) She works nights and isn't around during
        the day.
    (B) She is a very safe person.
    (C) I enjoyed meeting her, too.

13. Do you take the bus or the subway to work in
    the morning?
    (A) I also take the bus.
    (B) Yes, I've ridden the subway.
    (C) Usually the bus.

14. Are you really going out of business, Joe?
    (A) I'll open at three o'clock.
    (B) We don't take credit cards.
    (C) I've really got no choice.

15. When is the earnings forecast due out?
    (A) Mostly sunny this weekend.
    (B) Revenues declined last year.
    (C) It will be available next week.

16. When will you be able to take your vacation?
    (A) I will go to Guam for six days.
    (B) I'll be eligible after six months.
    (C) I had a wonderful time, thank you.

17. Sorry to bother you, but where is Pluton
    Electronics?
    (A) Third floor, second door on the left.
    (B) No trouble at all. Thanks.
    (C) No. I work for Veritek Electronics.

18. How is your new job working out?
    (A) I work out three times a week.
    (B) He's doing really well, thanks.
    (C) Well, honestly, not so good.

19. Why did they close the processing plant?
    (A) It's just for a month or so. They will do
        routine maintenance.
    (B) I've never really been good with plants.
        They take too much time and care.
    (C) The process is not that difficult once you get
        started.

20. Are you going to take the bigger desk or the
    desk near the window?
    (A) I'll buy the biggest window I can afford.
    (B) Probably not, it's too much work.
    (C) Well, the view is really good, so that should
        help me decide.

21. How long have you been retired?
    (A) Seven years now.
    (B) They need some air.
    (C) About three meters.

22. Is Central Bank somewhere around here?
    (A) It takes hard work to be a banker.
    (B) I'm looking for it, too.
    (C) We keep our money there, too.

23. Who was that man you were having lunch with the other day?
    (A) I had the shrimp salad.
    (B) That was a new client.
    (C) I eat there every Tuesday and Thursday.

24. When do you think the report will be done?
    (A) I can't be sure, but I think so.
    (B) Tomorrow, at the latest.
    (C) I saw it on her desk last week.

25. Where is my floppy disk?
    (A) I saw it next to your note pad.
    (B) Please return it when you are done.
    (C) Yes, the information on the disk was helpful.

26. What were the main points of the meeting?
    (A) The meeting was yesterday.
    (B) The man at the meeting was very knowledgeable.
    (C) It was about the company's budget, mostly.

27. How can I reach you?
    (A) I don't like to be touched.
    (B) I have a cell phone.
    (C) Richard left the building.

28. What did your attorney advise you to do?
    (A) She thinks I should file a suit.
    (B) The courtroom was quite full.
    (C) The judge hasn't ruled on it.

29. What do you think of the proposed merger?
    (A) I hope it doesn't take place.
    (B) I enjoyed it very much.
    (C) Both sides are considering it.

30. Why are you leaving your job?
    (A) Five o'clock. Time to go home.
    (B) I really like what I do for a living.
    (C) I got something that pays better.

31. Can we discuss it over lunch?
    (A) I'll have the tuna sandwich with pickles.
    (B) Sure, that'll be fine.
    (C) Of course, you're welcome to join us.

32. Do you want the good news first or the bad news?
    (A) Well, it's best to finish on a high note.
    (B) The newspaper is on my desk.
    (C) Why can't we have both?

33. Where is your boss? I don't see him around.
    (A) He's in a meeting right now.
    (B) Well, I don't mind either.
    (C) My boss has a good nose for business.

34. What is the phone number for the main office?
    (A) They should have a phone in their office.
    (B) They called this morning.
    (C) Check in the telephone directory.

35. Who here will sign for this package?
    (A) The package is on the table.
    (B) I'll go get someone.
    (C) It should be coming soon.

36. When did she start working here?
    (A) She will start tomorrow.
    (B) I don't really know.
    (C) She comes to work every day.

37. Can you take a message?
    (A) Sure. Where's a pen?
    (B) No, I'm going the opposite direction.
    (C) It's down the hall and on the left.

38. How did the interview go?
    (A) Not all that well.
    (B) I took the subway.
    (C) She's a movie star.

39. Who elects the corporate board of directors?
    (A) The stockholders do.
    (B) They have the right to vote.
    (C) They serve for a year.

40. Is transportation to the airport available?
    (A) It's nearly time to board the plane.
    (B) What is your reservation number?
    (C) We offer hourly shuttle bus service.

PART 3. Short Conversations

Questions 41 through 43 refer to the following conversation.

(M) Ms. Reed, have you read the chairman's memo? I think the information would be useful for your meeting with Westco tomorrow.
(W) Not yet, John. I've been busy reviewing sales numbers on the Turner account. The Turner account is due today, but Westco is still a day away.
(M) Just make sure that you give it a look before you meet with the team from Westco. I think the information will be useful for negotiating prices.

Questions 44 through 46 refer to the following conversation.

(M) Where do you buy your office equipment? Our office needs a new fax machine and photocopy machine, but we have a rather limited budget.

(W) I usually order it online. There are two really good wholesale office supply stores that ship free for orders over one thousand dollars. It's really easy to do.

(M) I've never ordered anything online before. If you have time could you show me how to do that?

Questions 47 through 49 refer to the following conversation.

(M) Has anyone found out what the vacation schedule is yet? I need to book an airplane ticket, but I don't know for which days yet.

(W) Peter told me the schedule, but I can't remember it exactly. I think our vacation starts on Thursday and finishes on the next Wednesday. I could be wrong, though.

(M) I need some definite dates. Will Peter be back from lunch anytime soon?

Questions 50 through 52 refer to the following conversation.

(W) Star Travel Agency. This is Miranda speaking.

(M) Hi Miranda. This is Tom from AdventureQuest. I just called to tell you that our tour of Guatemalan jungle temples is full, but we will be opening another tour of Machu Picchu in two months. Star Travel can book up to six people and take a 40% commission.

(W) Thanks, Tom. That's six for Machu Picchu. I'm sure it's going to be a popular tour.

Questions 53 through 55 refer to the following conversation.

(W) Ted, call the office and ask José to bring the projector. We'll need it for this afternoon's meeting. Also ask him to bring the big fold out table and the dais.

(M) Ann, José doesn't have a key to the equipment room. He hasn't been working here long enough to be given a key.

(W) Well, tell him there's one in my desk drawer. And tell Mrs. Ames to get José a key, he needs it to do his job.

Questions 56 through 58 refer to the following conversation.

(W) What have you heard from MegaStore? Do you know if you have the job?

(M) Not a thing. I haven't heard anything, and I've been waiting by the phone all morning. They must have hired someone else or they would have called by now.

(W) I doubt it. They probably don't see many résumés as impressive as yours. Especially all of your work experience.

(M) That's what I'm worried about. I think that I'm way overqualified.

Questions 59 through 61 refer to the following conversation.

(W) We missed you at yesterday's meeting. Were you ill? You really missed a lot of important information.

(M) I was fine, but there was a big problem in the product development department that kept me busy all day. It seems that the 10cm flange should have been only 1cm. Someone in engineering got the numbers wrong.

(W) Oh, man. That's bad. Does the big boss know?

(M) Not yet. I'm going to tell her right now.

Questions 62 through 64 refer to the following conversation.

(M) How is the new ad campaign going? It looks like it tested well with the 15 to 20 age group.

(W) Yeah, it did OK in the testing phase, but for some reason it doesn't seem to be doing well in real life.

(M) I had a feeling it wouldn't do so well. That singer that you got to do the ads isn't as popular as she was a few months ago when you were testing the ad campaign.

(W) Things change so quickly; it's hard to keep up with who's hot and who's not.

Questions 65 through 67 refer to the following conversation.

(W) Why is the factory shutting down? I thought it was doing really well.

(M) It was doing well until the price of steel went up. Now it is just too expensive to make anything. The factory is operating in the red and will close next month.

(W) I guess a lot of folks will be out of work. Practically this whole town has some family member working at the factory.

(M) Yeah, I know. My father and both of my brothers work there.

Questions 68 through 70 refer to the following conversation.

(W) Do you know why Louis resigned? He hadn't worked here even a year, and I thought that he liked his job.

(M) I guess the boss and he just didn't see eye to eye on a lot of things. I know that they disagreed on employee motivation strategies, among other things.

(W) Really? I thought they were getting along all right. They always seemed friendly towards each other.

(M) I think they were professional towards each other, not really friendly.

PART 4. Short Talks

Questions 71 through 73 refer to the following announcement.

(M) Ladies and gentlemen, I have two announcements relating to this afternoon's conference program. First, for those of you who were planning to attend Dr. Jennifer Van Dyke's lecture on marketing strategies, I'm afraid that I have some bad news: that event has been cancelled. The reason for this, unfortunately, is that Dr. Van Dyke must return to Australia because of a family emergency. I know that many of you will be disappointed, but I'm sure you understand the situation. The second thing I have for you is a room change. The location for the Personnel Management Seminar has been changed to conference room 6A. Let me repeat that, Dr Van Dyke's lecture will not be taking place today, and the two o'clock Personnel Management Seminar will be held in room 6A.

Questions 74 through 76 refer to the following announcement.

(W) Attention, travelers. We regret to inform you that because of a security situation, all entrances to and exits from Terminal D are temporarily closed. To repeat, airport patrons are currently not being allowed entry to or exit from Terminal D. If you are scheduled to board a flight from Terminal D, please report to an airline counter for further information. We would once again like to remind travelers to keep all baggage, including your children's, under your control at all times, and to notify the nearest security or airline official of any suspicious activity or unattended luggage. We apologize to all airport patrons for this inconvenience, but we are doing our best to make airline travel safer in these tense times.

Questions 77 through 79 refer to the following telephone message.

(M) This is Peter Kerensky, father of Olga Kerensky. Olga is a patient of Dr. Richards, and she has an appointment to see him tomorrow at nine. When Olga got her cast off last month, Dr. Richards told us to schedule another appointment and bring her back to see him if her wrist still hurt, but to go ahead and cancel it if not. So, that's what I'd like to do, cancel it, that is. It looks as though everything is OK, so we don't need to come. I'm sorry I didn't contact you earlier, but the truth is it just slipped my mind. Oh, and pass on my thanks to Dr. Richards for taking such good care of Olga's injury.

Questions 80 through 82 refer to the following short talk.

(W) Good morning, and welcome to your first day on the job at London Chemical, Ltd. As you know, this is the first of three days of orientation to the firm. First up today will be a welcoming address from our director of personnel, Dr. Ann Smiley, who will give you a broad overview of what you can expect in working for the firm, and what the firm expects of you. After Dr. Smiley's address, you will be given a tour of LC's headquarters and the central research facilities. Following the tour, you will have lunch in the main employee cafeteria, and be given a half-hour break before starting the afternoon program. Please note that attendance at all sessions is compulsory for all new employees, with no exceptions.

Questions 83 through 85 refer to the following announcement.

(M) Good afternoon ladies and gentlemen. This is your captain speaking. I'd like to welcome you aboard Green Island Airways Flight 287, bound for Auckland, with a stopover in Wellington. We are currently awaiting clearance for take-off, and should be in the air in just a few minutes. In the meantime, I'd like to remind you to do your part to make this a safe and enjoyable flight by keeping your seat belt on whenever you are in your seat. I am happy to inform you that the weather is quite a bit better in our destination cities than it is here in Bangkok: both Wellington and Auckland are reporting clear skies at the moment. I'd like you now to watch the following flight safety video. Please do not hesitate to ask any of our flight attendants if you have any needs or concerns.

Questions 86 through 88 refer to the following message.

(W) Thank you for calling Nautilus Copier. You have reached the Nautilus Copier support line. We are sorry but all of our technical representatives are currently assisting other customers. Calls will be handled in the order received. Your expected hold time is over five minutes, so we recommend that you call back at a more convenient time. If you choose to wait, please have the following information ready so that our representative may better assist you: your customer account number, the serial number of your copier, and your warranty expiration date, which may be found in the bottom right hand corner of your service agreement. We apologize for the wait, but assure you that one of our representatives will be with you as soon as possible.

(M) Welcome to the Tiger Falls International Visitors' Center. I am Mario, your guide for today's tour. As you may know, Tiger Falls is the fourth highest waterfall in the world. In just a few minutes, you will get an idea of just how high that is when we take the elevator to the caves located halfway down the falls. That ride will take about two full minutes, and when we get there, you will have the unforgettable experience of viewing the waterfall from the underside. That's right! We will be behind the falls themselves. You may get a little wet from the spray, so everybody will be getting a raincoat — unless, of course, you've brought your own.

(M) This is Pat King live in Boston with an update on that crash near Logan Airport. The plane went down early this morning and initial reports said that there were no survivors. Officials are now saying that these earlier reports may in fact have been premature. Once again, Condor Air officials are now expressing hope that there may in fact be survivors of the crash of one of their passenger craft in the waters near Logan airport. Although no one has been located yet, Peter Bush, senior spokesman for the company, has just told reporters that Coast Guard rescue helicopters have dropped divers into the waters near where the plane went down. Pat King, WBMB radio.

(W) Hello? This is Antonia Francis calling about the cake I said that I would be ordering. Well, I finally have the arrangements for the party settled, so I'd like to confirm some of the details we discussed before and to place a definite order. I want you to make a chocolate sponge cake, not a plain sponge as I previously mentioned. I'd like it to have a vanilla cream filling and a dark chocolate topping. It's up to you what shape or design the cake has, but it does need to be large enough for 50 people. It's for a 50th birthday party, so could you write "Happy Birthday Alan" on it? The party is on the 25th, so I'd like to have it delivered by 1:00 p.m. on the 25th. I'll drop by the store later to settle the bill. Thanks.

(M) As part of our new company efforts to encourage recycling and reduce waste, I am calling upon all of you to do your best to cooperate with the new garbage separation rules. I know that it is going to feel like a nuisance at first, but if you stick with it, it'll become quite a routine procedure. Remember, each of the four different types of garbage listed in the trash collection area goes in to a different receptacle. Papers go into the green box, cans and bottles go in the blue box, soft recyclable plastics such as candy wrappers and food containers go in the yellow box, and food waste should be put in the red box. If we can take home these habits, even better, but let's start by making every effort in the office.

PART 1

1. (D) The man is looking at papers.
2. (B) The office workers are looking at a whiteboard.
3. (C) The chef is working.
4. (A) There is no one in the store.
5. (C) The man is taking a phone call.
6. (D) The bicycle is between a tree and the stairs.
7. (B) The desk is a little untidy.
8. (B) The man is walking down the escalator.
9. (C) The ladder is leaning against the wall.
10. (B) A house is being built.

PART 2

11. (C) Usually, but not this week.
12. (A) Well, why don't we take a short break then?
13. (A) I'm not sure, I'll check.
14. (B) By express mail.
15. (C) Sure, I'll be there in just a second.
16. (B) I think it's a little unfair.
17. (B) Yes, absolutely brilliant.
18. (A) Neither, I'm flying there.
19. (C) It's on the fifth floor.
20. (B) I don't mind a little wait.
21. (A) I'd say the first woman we interviewed.
22. (B) No, I handle everything myself.
23. (C) Because we were instructed to.
24. (B) At the end of August.
25. (A) There's a taxi stand around the corner.
26. (A) I wanted to read them over dinner.
27. (A) I'm exhausted. Let's wait.
28. (B) I think it's already started.
29. (C) No, but they will be soon.
30. (C) Yes, unless something urgent comes up.
31. (A) Sure, it's C-R-U-Z.
32. (A) Sure, what time do you need it?
33. (B) No, I prefer safer investments.
34. (C) Store hours are the same all year.
35. (A) Personally, I like a good bargain sale.
36. (B) Any time after 10:00 should be OK.
37. (A) He called to say he's taking his son to the doctor.
38. (C) Just pull the green lever on the side.
39. (C) They're both good, but Blake is slightly cheaper.
40. (A) How does 3 o'clock sound?

PART 3

41. (B) A shipment of material
42. (B) The department store
43. (B) There was a mistake in the address.
44. (B) Trying to repair a computer
45. (D) The man has been doing the same task for a week.
46. (C) Before the end of the day
47. (A) She doesn't have enough cash on her.

48. (C) By check
49. (B) Two forms of identification
50. (C) It's a national holiday.
51. (D) He has a lot of work to catch up on.
52. (C) She will enjoy having a day off.
53. (A) He thinks he'll be late for work.
54. (B) Thirty minutes
55. (C) He'll get there in time.
56. (A) A telephone
57. (C) Both this store and the store next door
58. (C) She never lends it to customers.
59. (D) Near the woman
60. (B) Her brother
61. (A) The bus is cheaper.
62. (B) To have a coffee with John
63. (C) She is waiting on a phone call.
64. (D) A large coffee and a blueberry muffin
65. (B) Designs for a new building
66. (A) There are some mistakes in the structure of the building.
67. (C) An architectural firm
68. (A) There will be major changes made to the personnel department.
69. (D) He was offered a better job elsewhere.
70. (B) He pays too much attention to idle gossip.

PART 4

71. (B) A magazine editor
72. (C) 2 years
73. (A) She will answer questions.
74. (C) A car rental company
75. (A) Call another number
76. (D) Wednesday 10:00 p.m.
77. (A) The whole library will close.
78. (B) There is a maintenance problem.
79. (C) Telephone first
80. (C) Batteries
81. (A) While the light is flashing
82. (A) All sizes
83. (A) Once an hour
84. (D) Heavy rain continues to fall.
85. (A) They were injured.
86. (C) Radio show hosts
87. (B) Phone the radio station
88. (C) She will lose the chance to win some money.
89. (C) Five suspects
90. (B) For drug smuggling
91. (A) 25 years in prison
92. (B) The driver of a truck
93. (B) It will be towed off.
94. (B) In a parking lot across the street
95. (C) It operates in North America.
96. (C) Around three hours
97. (B) A food and beverage service
98. (B) The woman's son
99. (A) A pizza, vegetables, and ice cream
100. (C) Before eight o'clock.

PART 5

101. (B) of
102. (C) never
103. (C) regret
104. (A) ago
105. (A) unauthorized
106. (D) stacked
107. (D) Had
108. (B) ought
109. (B) oust
110. (B) revenue
111. (B) Like
112. (B) aide
113. (C) Almost
114. (A) should
115. (B) were
116. (A) off
117. (D) having
118. (C) alluded
119. (D) conceal
120. (A) whatever
121. (B) Hardly
122. (C) indeed
123. (D) rehearse
124. (C) her
125. (D) have had
126. (D) effect
127. (A) on
128. (D) has
129. (A) efficient
130. (B) is recommending
131. (C) provided
132. (A) would
133. (A) proceeds
134. (C) on
135. (A) few
136. (C) to provide
137. (C) is
138. (A) approve
139. (B) must
140. (C) rivals

PART 6

141. (B) loan
142. (C) deposited
143. (B) consultation
144. (C) will help
145. (B) a lot of
146. (A) aroused more
147. (D) discount
148. (D) look
149. (C) brought
150. (B) situation
151. (A) details
152. (D) supervisors

PART 7

153. (B) To cancel an order
154. (A) A contract to work for a private railway
155. (D) Max Green and John Andersen already know each other.
156. (A) In a changing room
157. (C) A series of numbers
158. (A) The Blue Wave has suffered thefts recently.
159. (C) Having lunch
160. (B) Some files
161. (D) She has been busy.
162. (B) To let Samantha know they have enough actors
163. (D) Five
164. (B) He wants to save money.
165. (B) Business people
166. (B) How to improve the speed of a computer
167. (C) Once a month
168. (B) Making your battery last longer
169. (A) To recruit a new engineer
170. (C) Four times a year
171. (D) Subsidized transportation
172. (C) People who previously applied for a job at Grant Manufacturing
173. (A) To get information about Patel Pottery's products
174. (B) They are rather expensive.
175. (C) Taking and dispatching orders
176. (D) By phone
177. (A) Because there have been several complaints from customers
178. (B) Someone who works on Thursdays and Fridays
179. (B) A tooth
180. (B) There is no mention of punishment in the memo.
181. (B) Once a year
182. (C) Chair of the Systems Advisory Committee
183. (A) Better communications and fewer errors
184. (D) Both John and Jenny attended the meeting.
185. (B) She wants him to check the accuracy of the minutes.
186. (B) To elicit feedback on an advertisement
187. (C) People in their twenties
188. (C) In April and May
189. (A) People might feel the company wants to attract only very young customers.
190. (B) Someone who enjoys nightclubs and parties
191. (B) He believed they had charged too much.
192. (A) A list of costs before doing repairs.
193. (A) Dispose of the old battery
194. (C) Nothing
195. (B) It is very good.
196. (A) Sales results
197. (A) About 40
198. (C) People need more space to store food for holiday guests.
199. (D) Washing machines
200. (B) Groceries

PRACTICE TEST 2

PART 1

1. (B) The woman is leaning on the pillar.
2. (B) The filing cabinet is open.
3. (D) The woman is working in her office.
4. (C) The restaurant is closed.
5. (A) The man and woman are talking.
6. (A) The man and woman are being served by the waitress.
7. (C) There are cars parked in front of the shopping mall.
8. (A) The people are pointing at the form.
9. (A) The man is standing in a supermarket.
10. (B) There is a large vase on the table in the lobby.

PART 2

11. (B) Down the hall and to the right.
12. (A) She works nights and isn't around during the day.
13. (C) Usually the bus.
14. (C) I've really got no choice.
15. (C) It will be available next week.
16. (B) I'll be eligible after six months.
17. (A) Third floor, second door on the left.
18. (C) Well, honestly, not so good.
19. (A) It's just for a month or so. They will do routine maintenance.
20. (C) Well, the view is really good, so that should help me decide.
21. (A) Seven years now.
22. (B) I'm looking for it, too.
23. (B) That was a new client.
24. (B) Tomorrow, at the latest.
25. (A) I saw it next to your note pad.
26. (C) It was about the company's budget, mostly.
27. (B) I have a cell phone.
28. (A) She thinks I should file a suit.
29. (A) I hope it doesn't take place.
30. (C) I got something that pays better.
31. (B) Sure, that'll be fine.
32. (A) Well, it's best to finish on a high note.
33. (A) He's in a meeting right now.
34. (C) Check in the telephone directory.
35. (B) I'll go get someone.
36. (B) I don't really know.
37. (A) Sure. Where's a pen?
38. (A) Not all that well.
39. (A) The stockholders do.
40. (C) We offer hourly shuttle bus service.

PART 3

41. (B) John
42. (C) It will help to negotiate prices.
43. (A) The Turner account
44. (A) A fax machine and a copy machine
45. (D) From an online wholesale supplier
46. (C) $1,000.00

47. (C) The vacation schedule
48. (A) At lunch
49. (C) To book an airline ticket
50. (B) Their companies sometimes work together.
51. (B) Forty percent
52. (D) Many people will be interested in it.
53. (A) A projector, a table, and a dais
54. (D) He doesn't have a key.
55. (C) Ann
56. (C) By phone
57. (B) He has a lot of work experience.
58. (D) He is overqualified.
59. (C) Yesterday
60. (A) Product Development
61. (C) Talk to his boss
62. (D) Fifteen to twenty years of age
63. (B) A singer
64. (C) The singer is no longer popular.
65. (B) The cost of raw materials has gone up.
66. (C) Next month
67. (A) Three
68. (A) Less than one year
69. (C) How employees should be motivated
70. (D) They kept a professional attitude even if they weren't friends.

PART 4

71. (A) Preparing to return to Australia
72. (B) It has been moved to room 6A.
73. (A) 2
74. (B) An unattended bag was found.
75. (B) Those waiting to depart from Terminal D.
76. (B) Security or airline officials
77. (A) A hurt wrist
78. (D) He had simply forgotten about it.
79. (B) Her injury is no longer bothering her.
80. (C) The head of personnel
81. (A) The morning's agenda
82. (D) The company headquarters
83. (A) Auckland
84. (A) Use their seatbelts
85. (B) The passengers will watch a safety video.
86. (C) Copier owners experiencing problems
87. (B) The hold time is quite long.
88. (A) The warranty expiration date
89. (C) Three
90. (D) Viewing the falls from the underside
91. (D) Tourists who have brought their own
92. (C) The radio reported on the crash earlier.
93. (D) It is not known.
94. (B) Over the sea
95. (C) A bakery
96. (A) Antonia has already paid for the cake.
97. (A) Antonia has contacted the store before.
98. (C) A new trash collection system
99. (C) Four
100. (B) An empty soda can

PART 5

101. (C) complaining
102. (B) would
103. (C) claustrophobia
104. (C) lure
105. (D) As far as
106. (D) discriminatory
107. (D) would
108. (A) wages
109. (D) frustration
110. (A) tariffs
111. (B) expense
112. (A) pension
113. (B) observing
114. (A) behalf
115. (D) receptionist
116. (C) or else
117. (B) response
118. (A) audit
119. (C) promoted
120. (A) did not
121. (C) spacious
122. (A) satisfaction
123. (B) don't mind
124. (D) consider
125. (D) but
126. (C) themselves
127. (B) Advertising
128. (D) gave
129. (A) is
130. (D) has
131. (D) is
132. (A) on
133. (D) lavatory
134. (B) really
135. (D) log out
136. (B) paychecks
137. (A) better
138. (D) am
139. (C) earpiece
140. (B) salary

PART 6

141. (C) attention
142. (A) due
143. (D) efforts
144. (A) file
145. (D) inform
146. (B) purchasing
147. (A) invite
148. (C) occasion
149. (C) opening
150. (A) running
151. (B) down
152. (C) serving

PART 7

153. (C) To support Lydia Rivers' application for a loan
154. (B) Dr. Rivers may be able to borrow money from a bank.
155. (B) Novino
156. (C) SunCool is sold in more than one country.
157. (B) One is more likely to win a car than a motorcycle.
158. (B) Someone born in November, 1995
159. (A) The amount of money expected to be raised
160. (C) A fund-raiser to help poorer schoolchildren
161. (B) On a summer morning
162. (A) That they be taken the day before being submitted
163. (C) The head of the applicant must be shown bare.
164. (A) The application number
165. (B) Included with purchased software
166. (B) "Spend hours memorizing historical dates!"
167. (A) Software engineers
168. (C) CompuEd products have won awards in the past.
169. (A) It is $6.00 per hour.
170. (C) Only a limited number of positions will be filled.
171. (B) Residents of Steuben County
172. (B) Fifteen
173. (D) Costas Workers Start Strike Today
174. (B) An offer by the company that the union found unacceptable
175. (C) Indefinitely
176. (C) The economy of the community would suffer.
177. (B) Employees of Food Mart
178. (A) Around 10 days
179. (A) The north parking lot
180. (B) People are taking things out of them.
181. (A) To discuss an order of clothes
182. (B) There is a great demand for them.
183. (B) They are busy fulfilling other orders.
184. (B) Telephoning manufacturers and suppliers
185. (D) It is very doubtful.
186. (B) To ask for her money back
187. (D) She is a loyal customer of Hanley Electronics.
188. (B) A total of 10 minutes
189. (A) None for this particular product
190. (C) Name, address, and reference number
191. (C) To express concern about the downtown retail area
192. (B) A member of an organization concerned with protecting small businesses
193. (C) In 2005, only coffee shops seem to have remained successful downtown.
194. (D) Rising crime
195. (A) Stimulate the downtown area and limit out-of-town retail areas
196. (A) To recruit a cook
197. (C) It has relatively new equipment in the kitchen.
198. (C) He wants more responsibility.
199. (B) An independent, cooperative person with a few years experience
200. (B) Making deliveries

ANSWER SHEET

PRACTICE TEST 1

LISTENING (Parts 1 – 4)

NO.	ANSWER	NO.	ANSWER	NO.	ANSWER	NO.	ANSWER	NO.	ANSWER
	A B C D		A B C D		A B C D		A B C D		A B C D
1	ⓐⓑⓒⓓ	21	ⓐⓑⓒⓓ	41	ⓐⓑⓒⓓ	61	ⓐⓑⓒⓓ	81	ⓐⓑⓒⓓ
2	ⓐⓑⓒⓓ	22	ⓐⓑⓒⓓ	42	ⓐⓑⓒⓓ	62	ⓐⓑⓒⓓ	82	ⓐⓑⓒⓓ
3	ⓐⓑⓒⓓ	23	ⓐⓑⓒⓓ	43	ⓐⓑⓒⓓ	63	ⓐⓑⓒⓓ	83	ⓐⓑⓒⓓ
4	ⓐⓑⓒⓓ	24	ⓐⓑⓒⓓ	44	ⓐⓑⓒⓓ	64	ⓐⓑⓒⓓ	84	ⓐⓑⓒⓓ
5	ⓐⓑⓒⓓ	25	ⓐⓑⓒⓓ	45	ⓐⓑⓒⓓ	65	ⓐⓑⓒⓓ	85	ⓐⓑⓒⓓ
6	ⓐⓑⓒⓓ	26	ⓐⓑⓒⓓ	46	ⓐⓑⓒⓓ	66	ⓐⓑⓒⓓ	86	ⓐⓑⓒⓓ
7	ⓐⓑⓒⓓ	27	ⓐⓑⓒⓓ	47	ⓐⓑⓒⓓ	67	ⓐⓑⓒⓓ	87	ⓐⓑⓒⓓ
8	ⓐⓑⓒⓓ	28	ⓐⓑⓒⓓ	48	ⓐⓑⓒⓓ	68	ⓐⓑⓒⓓ	88	ⓐⓑⓒⓓ
9	ⓐⓑⓒⓓ	29	ⓐⓑⓒⓓ	49	ⓐⓑⓒⓓ	69	ⓐⓑⓒⓓ	89	ⓐⓑⓒⓓ
10	ⓐⓑⓒⓓ	30	ⓐⓑⓒⓓ	50	ⓐⓑⓒⓓ	70	ⓐⓑⓒⓓ	90	ⓐⓑⓒⓓ
11	ⓐⓑⓒⓓ	31	ⓐⓑⓒⓓ	51	ⓐⓑⓒⓓ	71	ⓐⓑⓒⓓ	91	ⓐⓑⓒⓓ
12	ⓐⓑⓒⓓ	32	ⓐⓑⓒⓓ	52	ⓐⓑⓒⓓ	72	ⓐⓑⓒⓓ	92	ⓐⓑⓒⓓ
13	ⓐⓑⓒⓓ	33	ⓐⓑⓒⓓ	53	ⓐⓑⓒⓓ	73	ⓐⓑⓒⓓ	93	ⓐⓑⓒⓓ
14	ⓐⓑⓒⓓ	34	ⓐⓑⓒⓓ	54	ⓐⓑⓒⓓ	74	ⓐⓑⓒⓓ	94	ⓐⓑⓒⓓ
15	ⓐⓑⓒⓓ	35	ⓐⓑⓒⓓ	55	ⓐⓑⓒⓓ	75	ⓐⓑⓒⓓ	95	ⓐⓑⓒⓓ
16	ⓐⓑⓒⓓ	36	ⓐⓑⓒⓓ	56	ⓐⓑⓒⓓ	76	ⓐⓑⓒⓓ	96	ⓐⓑⓒⓓ
17	ⓐⓑⓒⓓ	37	ⓐⓑⓒⓓ	57	ⓐⓑⓒⓓ	77	ⓐⓑⓒⓓ	97	ⓐⓑⓒⓓ
18	ⓐⓑⓒⓓ	38	ⓐⓑⓒⓓ	58	ⓐⓑⓒⓓ	78	ⓐⓑⓒⓓ	98	ⓐⓑⓒⓓ
19	ⓐⓑⓒⓓ	39	ⓐⓑⓒⓓ	59	ⓐⓑⓒⓓ	79	ⓐⓑⓒⓓ	99	ⓐⓑⓒⓓ
20	ⓐⓑⓒⓓ	40	ⓐⓑⓒⓓ	60	ⓐⓑⓒⓓ	80	ⓐⓑⓒⓓ	100	ⓐⓑⓒⓓ

READING (Parts 5 – 7)

NO.	ANSWER	NO.	ANSWER	NO.	ANSWER	NO.	ANSWER	NO.	ANSWER
	A B C D		A B C D		A B C D		A B C D		A B C D
101	ⓐⓑⓒⓓ	121	ⓐⓑⓒⓓ	141	ⓐⓑⓒⓓ	161	ⓐⓑⓒⓓ	181	ⓐⓑⓒⓓ
102	ⓐⓑⓒⓓ	122	ⓐⓑⓒⓓ	142	ⓐⓑⓒⓓ	162	ⓐⓑⓒⓓ	182	ⓐⓑⓒⓓ
103	ⓐⓑⓒⓓ	123	ⓐⓑⓒⓓ	143	ⓐⓑⓒⓓ	163	ⓐⓑⓒⓓ	183	ⓐⓑⓒⓓ
104	ⓐⓑⓒⓓ	124	ⓐⓑⓒⓓ	144	ⓐⓑⓒⓓ	164	ⓐⓑⓒⓓ	184	ⓐⓑⓒⓓ
105	ⓐⓑⓒⓓ	125	ⓐⓑⓒⓓ	145	ⓐⓑⓒⓓ	165	ⓐⓑⓒⓓ	185	ⓐⓑⓒⓓ
106	ⓐⓑⓒⓓ	126	ⓐⓑⓒⓓ	146	ⓐⓑⓒⓓ	166	ⓐⓑⓒⓓ	186	ⓐⓑⓒⓓ
107	ⓐⓑⓒⓓ	127	ⓐⓑⓒⓓ	147	ⓐⓑⓒⓓ	167	ⓐⓑⓒⓓ	187	ⓐⓑⓒⓓ
108	ⓐⓑⓒⓓ	128	ⓐⓑⓒⓓ	148	ⓐⓑⓒⓓ	168	ⓐⓑⓒⓓ	188	ⓐⓑⓒⓓ
109	ⓐⓑⓒⓓ	129	ⓐⓑⓒⓓ	149	ⓐⓑⓒⓓ	169	ⓐⓑⓒⓓ	189	ⓐⓑⓒⓓ
110	ⓐⓑⓒⓓ	130	ⓐⓑⓒⓓ	150	ⓐⓑⓒⓓ	170	ⓐⓑⓒⓓ	190	ⓐⓑⓒⓓ
111	ⓐⓑⓒⓓ	131	ⓐⓑⓒⓓ	151	ⓐⓑⓒⓓ	171	ⓐⓑⓒⓓ	191	ⓐⓑⓒⓓ
112	ⓐⓑⓒⓓ	132	ⓐⓑⓒⓓ	152	ⓐⓑⓒⓓ	172	ⓐⓑⓒⓓ	192	ⓐⓑⓒⓓ
113	ⓐⓑⓒⓓ	133	ⓐⓑⓒⓓ	153	ⓐⓑⓒⓓ	173	ⓐⓑⓒⓓ	193	ⓐⓑⓒⓓ
114	ⓐⓑⓒⓓ	134	ⓐⓑⓒⓓ	154	ⓐⓑⓒⓓ	174	ⓐⓑⓒⓓ	194	ⓐⓑⓒⓓ
115	ⓐⓑⓒⓓ	135	ⓐⓑⓒⓓ	155	ⓐⓑⓒⓓ	175	ⓐⓑⓒⓓ	195	ⓐⓑⓒⓓ
116	ⓐⓑⓒⓓ	136	ⓐⓑⓒⓓ	156	ⓐⓑⓒⓓ	176	ⓐⓑⓒⓓ	196	ⓐⓑⓒⓓ
117	ⓐⓑⓒⓓ	137	ⓐⓑⓒⓓ	157	ⓐⓑⓒⓓ	177	ⓐⓑⓒⓓ	197	ⓐⓑⓒⓓ
118	ⓐⓑⓒⓓ	138	ⓐⓑⓒⓓ	158	ⓐⓑⓒⓓ	178	ⓐⓑⓒⓓ	198	ⓐⓑⓒⓓ
119	ⓐⓑⓒⓓ	139	ⓐⓑⓒⓓ	159	ⓐⓑⓒⓓ	179	ⓐⓑⓒⓓ	199	ⓐⓑⓒⓓ
120	ⓐⓑⓒⓓ	140	ⓐⓑⓒⓓ	160	ⓐⓑⓒⓓ	180	ⓐⓑⓒⓓ	200	ⓐⓑⓒⓓ

ANSWER SHEET

PRACTICE TEST 2

LISTENING (Parts 1 – 4)

NO.	ANSWER	NO.	ANSWER	NO.	ANSWER	NO.	ANSWER
	A B C D		A B C D		A B C D		A B C D
1	ⓐⓑⓒ	21	ⓐⓑⓒⓓ	41	ⓐⓑⓒⓓ	61	ⓐⓑⓒⓓ
2	ⓐⓑⓒ	22	ⓐⓑⓒⓓ	42	ⓐⓑⓒⓓ	62	ⓐⓑⓒⓓ
3	ⓐⓑⓒ	23	ⓐⓑⓒⓓ	43	ⓐⓑⓒⓓ	63	ⓐⓑⓒⓓ
4	ⓐⓑⓒ	24	ⓐⓑⓒⓓ	44	ⓐⓑⓒⓓ	64	ⓐⓑⓒⓓ
5	ⓐⓑⓒ	25	ⓐⓑⓒⓓ	45	ⓐⓑⓒⓓ	65	ⓐⓑⓒⓓ
6	ⓐⓑⓒ	26	ⓐⓑⓒⓓ	46	ⓐⓑⓒⓓ	66	ⓐⓑⓒⓓ
7	ⓐⓑⓒ	27	ⓐⓑⓒⓓ	47	ⓐⓑⓒⓓ	67	ⓐⓑⓒⓓ
8	ⓐⓑⓒ	28	ⓐⓑⓒⓓ	48	ⓐⓑⓒⓓ	68	ⓐⓑⓒⓓ
9	ⓐⓑⓒ	29	ⓐⓑⓒⓓ	49	ⓐⓑⓒⓓ	69	ⓐⓑⓒⓓ
10	ⓐⓑⓒ	30	ⓐⓑⓒⓓ	50	ⓐⓑⓒⓓ	70	ⓐⓑⓒⓓ
11	ⓐⓑⓒ	31	ⓐⓑⓒⓓ	51	ⓐⓑⓒⓓ	71	ⓐⓑⓒⓓ
12	ⓐⓑⓒ	32	ⓐⓑⓒⓓ	52	ⓐⓑⓒⓓ	72	ⓐⓑⓒⓓ
13	ⓐⓑⓒ	33	ⓐⓑⓒⓓ	53	ⓐⓑⓒⓓ	73	ⓐⓑⓒⓓ
14	ⓐⓑⓒ	34	ⓐⓑⓒⓓ	54	ⓐⓑⓒⓓ	74	ⓐⓑⓒⓓ
15	ⓐⓑⓒ	35	ⓐⓑⓒⓓ	55	ⓐⓑⓒⓓ	75	ⓐⓑⓒⓓ
16	ⓐⓑⓒ	36	ⓐⓑⓒⓓ	56	ⓐⓑⓒⓓ	76	ⓐⓑⓒⓓ
17	ⓐⓑⓒ	37	ⓐⓑⓒⓓ	57	ⓐⓑⓒⓓ	77	ⓐⓑⓒⓓ
18	ⓐⓑⓒ	38	ⓐⓑⓒⓓ	58	ⓐⓑⓒⓓ	78	ⓐⓑⓒⓓ
19	ⓐⓑⓒ	39	ⓐⓑⓒⓓ	59	ⓐⓑⓒⓓ	79	ⓐⓑⓒⓓ
20	ⓐⓑⓒ	40	ⓐⓑⓒⓓ	60	ⓐⓑⓒⓓ	80	ⓐⓑⓒⓓ

NO.	ANSWER
	A B C D
81	ⓐⓑⓒⓓ
82	ⓐⓑⓒⓓ
83	ⓐⓑⓒⓓ
84	ⓐⓑⓒⓓ
85	ⓐⓑⓒⓓ
86	ⓐⓑⓒⓓ
87	ⓐⓑⓒⓓ
88	ⓐⓑⓒⓓ
89	ⓐⓑⓒⓓ
90	ⓐⓑⓒⓓ
91	ⓐⓑⓒⓓ
92	ⓐⓑⓒⓓ
93	ⓐⓑⓒⓓ
94	ⓐⓑⓒⓓ
95	ⓐⓑⓒⓓ
96	ⓐⓑⓒⓓ
97	ⓐⓑⓒⓓ
98	ⓐⓑⓒⓓ
99	ⓐⓑⓒⓓ
100	ⓐⓑⓒⓓ

READING (Parts 5 – 7)

NO.	ANSWER	NO.	ANSWER	NO.	ANSWER	NO.	ANSWER	NO.	ANSWER
	A B C D		A B C D		A B C D		A B C D		A B C D
101	ⓐⓑⓒⓓ	121	ⓐⓑⓒⓓ	141	ⓐⓑⓒⓓ	161	ⓐⓑⓒⓓ	181	ⓐⓑⓒⓓ
102	ⓐⓑⓒⓓ	122	ⓐⓑⓒⓓ	142	ⓐⓑⓒⓓ	162	ⓐⓑⓒⓓ	182	ⓐⓑⓒⓓ
103	ⓐⓑⓒⓓ	123	ⓐⓑⓒⓓ	143	ⓐⓑⓒⓓ	163	ⓐⓑⓒⓓ	183	ⓐⓑⓒⓓ
104	ⓐⓑⓒⓓ	124	ⓐⓑⓒⓓ	144	ⓐⓑⓒⓓ	164	ⓐⓑⓒⓓ	184	ⓐⓑⓒⓓ
105	ⓐⓑⓒⓓ	125	ⓐⓑⓒⓓ	145	ⓐⓑⓒⓓ	165	ⓐⓑⓒⓓ	185	ⓐⓑⓒⓓ
106	ⓐⓑⓒⓓ	126	ⓐⓑⓒⓓ	146	ⓐⓑⓒⓓ	166	ⓐⓑⓒⓓ	186	ⓐⓑⓒⓓ
107	ⓐⓑⓒⓓ	127	ⓐⓑⓒⓓ	147	ⓐⓑⓒⓓ	167	ⓐⓑⓒⓓ	187	ⓐⓑⓒⓓ
108	ⓐⓑⓒⓓ	128	ⓐⓑⓒⓓ	148	ⓐⓑⓒⓓ	168	ⓐⓑⓒⓓ	188	ⓐⓑⓒⓓ
109	ⓐⓑⓒⓓ	129	ⓐⓑⓒⓓ	149	ⓐⓑⓒⓓ	169	ⓐⓑⓒⓓ	189	ⓐⓑⓒⓓ
110	ⓐⓑⓒⓓ	130	ⓐⓑⓒⓓ	150	ⓐⓑⓒⓓ	170	ⓐⓑⓒⓓ	190	ⓐⓑⓒⓓ
111	ⓐⓑⓒⓓ	131	ⓐⓑⓒⓓ	151	ⓐⓑⓒⓓ	171	ⓐⓑⓒⓓ	191	ⓐⓑⓒⓓ
112	ⓐⓑⓒⓓ	132	ⓐⓑⓒⓓ	152	ⓐⓑⓒⓓ	172	ⓐⓑⓒⓓ	192	ⓐⓑⓒⓓ
113	ⓐⓑⓒⓓ	133	ⓐⓑⓒⓓ	153	ⓐⓑⓒⓓ	173	ⓐⓑⓒⓓ	193	ⓐⓑⓒⓓ
114	ⓐⓑⓒⓓ	134	ⓐⓑⓒⓓ	154	ⓐⓑⓒⓓ	174	ⓐⓑⓒⓓ	194	ⓐⓑⓒⓓ
115	ⓐⓑⓒⓓ	135	ⓐⓑⓒⓓ	155	ⓐⓑⓒⓓ	175	ⓐⓑⓒⓓ	195	ⓐⓑⓒⓓ
116	ⓐⓑⓒⓓ	136	ⓐⓑⓒⓓ	156	ⓐⓑⓒⓓ	176	ⓐⓑⓒⓓ	196	ⓐⓑⓒⓓ
117	ⓐⓑⓒⓓ	137	ⓐⓑⓒⓓ	157	ⓐⓑⓒⓓ	177	ⓐⓑⓒⓓ	197	ⓐⓑⓒⓓ
118	ⓐⓑⓒⓓ	138	ⓐⓑⓒⓓ	158	ⓐⓑⓒⓓ	178	ⓐⓑⓒⓓ	198	ⓐⓑⓒⓓ
119	ⓐⓑⓒⓓ	139	ⓐⓑⓒⓓ	159	ⓐⓑⓒⓓ	179	ⓐⓑⓒⓓ	199	ⓐⓑⓒⓓ
120	ⓐⓑⓒⓓ	140	ⓐⓑⓒⓓ	160	ⓐⓑⓒⓓ	180	ⓐⓑⓒⓓ	200	ⓐⓑⓒⓓ